THE
PORNOGRAPHY
OF POWER

BOOKS BY ROBERT SCHEER

*Playing President: My Close Encounters with Nixon, Carter,
Bush I, Reagan, and Clinton—and How They
Did Not Prepare Me for George W. Bush*

The Five Biggest Lies Bush Told Us about Iraq
(coauthors Christopher Scheer and Lakshmi Chaudhry)

*Thinking Tuna Fish, Talking Death:
Essays on the Pornography of Power*

With Enough Shovels: Reagan, Bush & Nuclear War

America after Nixon: The Age of the Multinationals

Cuba: Tragedy in Our Hemisphere
(coauthor Maurice Zeitlin)

How the United States Got Involved in Vietnam

EDITED BY ROBERT SCHEER

The Cosmetic Surgery Revolution

*Eldridge Cleaver: Post-Prison Writings and
Speeches by the Author of* Soul on Ice

The Diary of Che Guevara

THE PORNOGRAPHY OF POWER

Why Defense Spending Must Be Cut

ROBERT SCHEER

NEW YORK  BOSTON

TWELVE

Twelve
Hachette Book Group
237 Park Avenue
New York, NY 10017

Visit our Web site at www.HachetteBookGroup.com.

Twelve is an imprint of Grand Central Publishing.
The Twelve name and logo are trademarks of Hachette Book Group, Inc.

Book design by Fearn Cutler de Vicq

Printed in the United States of America

Originally published in hardcover by Twelve.

FIRST TRADE EDITION: JUNE 2009
10 9 8 7 6 5 4 3 2 1

The Library of Congress has cataloged the hardcover edition as follows:
Scheer, Robert.
The pornography of power : how defense hawks hijacked 9/11 and
weakened America / Robert Scheer.
    p. cm.
Includes index.
ISBN: 978-0-446-50527-7
    1. Pentagon (Va.)   2. United States. Dept. of Defense.   3. Militarism—
United States—History—21st century.   4. September 11 Terrorist Attacks,
2001.   I. Title.
UA23.S4164   2008
973.931—dc22
                                    2008000375
ISBN 978-0-446-50526-0 (pbk.)

To Dwight David Eisenhower and George McGovern,
two war heroes who preferred plowshares to swords

CONTENTS

PROLOGUE

It was odd to be with Richard Nixon alone. Odder yet that what he had to say made so much sense, more than the four other presidents I have interviewed. While I can't quite bring myself to dedicate this book to Nixon—after all, I did witness the murderous consequences of his Indochinese bombing campaign up close—I have to admit that the ideas he expressed to me in an interview for the *Los Angeles Times*, eleven years after he was forced from office, resonate throughout this book.

The discussion here focuses on the limits of American power in a multipolar world and the disutility of our incredibly expensive military arsenal. Nixon's resignation in disgrace as a result of the Watergate scandal, deserved as that punishment was, and his mindless escalation of the Vietnam War he had inherited from Lyndon Johnson, obscured his real achievements in negotiating arms control and a new era of détente with the communist giants.

Earlier, as editor of *Ramparts* magazine, I had experienced his dark side, as I would learn in greater detail later from files released under a court order issued by Federal Judge Cecil Poole, a quite terrific Northern California jurist. The thousands of pages of documents revealed use of Nixon's FBI and CIA for several years to harass me and *Ramparts*. What irony that Nixon was cozying up to bloody communist tyrants abroad while harassing quite benign leftists here at home. He did try to put Daniel Ellsberg away for life for the crime of letting Americans read the Pentagon's Vietnam study, for which they paid with their tax dollars.

So, I had my issues with the man. Yet it occurred to me, four years into the presidency of Ronald Reagan, that Nixon's foreign policy seemed quite enlightened in comparison to that of the incumbent, or of Jimmy Carter, and I wrote that in an article for the *Times*. I noted that Nixon, although he escalated the Vietnam War, also had undermined the basic assumptions of the larger Cold War. Nixon read the article and agreed. In a friendly note, he thanked me for "very objective and comprehensive coverage of some of my activities," and then added, "I would like to arrange a mutually convenient time when you are in the New York area for a discussion of the origination of some of my foreign policy initiatives." I couldn't refuse.

I met with Nixon in June 1984, in his office in the federal building in lower Manhattan. He first spoke of topics—surfing on California beaches and the recent birth of his granddaughter—that veered far from the foreign policy issues to which he had restricted the interview. He appeared relaxed, though seated formally behind his massive desk. He was surrounded by photographs of himself with heads of state, a fitting setting for our discussion.

The grizzled warmonger had come, over the years, to recognize that the "enemy" was not the devil, and that communism—the all-too-convenient bête noire evoked during the early decades of his political life—was neither monolithic nor incapable of change: "I've always had a more subtle approach to the Soviet bloc—never have seen it as monolithic." Not quite true, but this is Nixon I'm quoting.

To make his point, Nixon noted his recognition of communist regime attitude changes like "night and day because of contacts with the West." He cited in particular his early support for Tito's Yugoslavia as that communist-led country broke with the Soviets, changes in Hungary, and of course his historic opening to China and pursuit of détente with the Soviet Union. I need not point out that Nixon was hardly naive about the persistent authoritarian rule in those countries, but he called for, as he put it in our discussion, a "live and let live" middle ground as represented by his willingness to negotiate as well as to confront.

I bring it up now because one cannot understand the neocon ideologues who came to dominate U.S. policy after 9/11 without understanding that they first came into existence in deeply traumatic opposition to Nixon and his policy of détente with the enemy.

For younger readers, it may be difficult to grasp the hold that an incredibly simplistic fear that something routinely referred to as "international communism and its timetable for the takeover of the world" instilled in our national political imagination. Like the post-9/11 "global war on terror," the fight against international communism was a construct driven as much by fear of being attacked as unpatriotic—a legacy in part of Nixon's own early smear campaigns against opponents he labeled as "soft on communism"—as it was by genuine conviction. That was certainly true of centrist and liberal politicians and intellectuals who signed on for those crusades, past and present, knowing full well that the basic argument was flawed.

Ironically, Nixon, the original demagogue on this point,

changed course earlier than many of those he had bludgeoned into going along with the rhetoric of the Cold War. But he had changed largely as a result of serving as Dwight Eisenhower's vice president, during which time Nixon had met the enemy and, in one famous Moscow kitchen debate, outtalked him. Nixon outflanked many of his critics in the Democratic Party by becoming reasonable, a sharp reversal of his earlier self.

A year before he became president, Nixon wrote a myth-shattering article for *Foreign Affairs* magazine advocating negotiations with Communist China, and to the degree that it was noticed in the media, it was dismissed as posturing for a future presidential campaign; but Nixon had meant it.

The picture of him as president chatting amiably with Mao Tse-tung, thought until then to be the bloodiest dictator of them all, and then having his secretary of state, Henry Kissinger, begin to negotiate with Chou En-lai on the specifics of a new U.S.–China embrace alarmed the Cold War hardliners back in the United States. The Cold War may have thawed, but a new one between "realists" and "neocons" had begun.

A number of the key neocons, including Richard Perle and Paul Wolfowitz, worked for Henry "Scoop" Jackson, the hawkish Democrat in thrall to the Boeing Company, the large aerospace contractor based in his home state of Washington. The alliance between the threat-inflating ideologues continuously sounding the alarm about an ever more menacing enemy and the needs of a military-industrial complex that required such an enemy in order to secure ever larger contracts was a constant feature of the Cold War years. In the debates over Nixon's policy of détente, the alliance between the defense intellectuals and the war profiteers came into clearest view.

At the core of the dispute was the perceived role of the United States as a power in the world. For Nixon and his ideological mentor in these matters, Dwight Eisenhower, whom he served faithfully as vice president, a multipolar world was a given. Eisenhower had been the victorious commander of a genuine international effort, and even though our World War II allies, particularly France, which was a government in exile, and England, battered by bombs, were militarily weakened, they were treated with great respect. Though the Soviets moved from ally to enemy, the Eisenhower administration never gave up the prospect of bringing them back into the fold through negotiation. It was Eisenhower, more than anyone, who deserves credit for the unraveling of the Cold War by bringing Nikita Khrushchev to the United States to view and envy the bountiful grain fields of capitalist Kansas.

Nixon, for all of the anticommunist rhetoric of his early years, followed in Eisenhower's footsteps. The war in Vietnam, which he murderously escalated, had been started by Democratic President John F. Kennedy and advanced to the point of madness by Lyndon Johnson. Yet, while continuing the fight against communism in Vietnam, Nixon undermined the basic tenet of the Cold War by entering into détente with the two megacommunist nations. For that, the neocons never forgave him.

Explaining both his détente with the Soviets and his equally historically significant opening to Communist China, Nixon told me: "I thought it was very important to recognize that the world is multipolar, not bipolar, and the more multipolar, the better it is for the United States."

That one sentence best summarizes the worldview of Nixon, Ford, Carter, Bush I, and Clinton. It was not the view of Reagan, who came into office stressing the unique obligation of the U.S. pole, or the biblically ordained "City on a Hill," as he would refer to America. But by the end of his term, Reagan had softened considerably, as evidenced by his opening to Mikhail

Gorbachev, where for a brief moment, both leaders agreed to abolish nuclear weapons.

Ever since Ronald Reagan had his meeting with Gorbachev in Reykjavík, Iceland, in October 1986, I assumed that the Cold War was over, and with it the excuse for massive military spending. Certainly after the first President Bush announced deep cuts in the Defense Department budget, I shared the general expectation of a "peace dividend" now that there was no longer a serious enemy in sight.

During the decade before September 11, 2001, it would never have occurred to me to write a book about the military-industrial complex, given the sudden collapse of the Soviet enemy that had justified its existence. For thirty years, mostly as a reporter and columnist for the *Los Angeles Times*, I had covered the Cold War arms race, at times exposing the excesses in spending and the contradictions in policy making while acknowledging that the United States was indeed up against a militarily formidable enemy, justifying an adequate response in U.S. weaponry and force structures. But then came Gorbachev, and with him the end of the Soviet empire. The clouds of war parted unexpectedly and the end of a permanent wartime economy and the long-awaited peace dividend seemed at hand.

As George H. W. Bush put it in his 1992 State of the Union Address, "I'm not sure we've absorbed the full impact, the full import of what happened. But communism died this year." He then went on to utter words that sent a shiver through the military-industrial complex that had solidified its claim on the federal budget spanning half a century:

> I mean to speak this evening of the changes
> that can take place in our country, now that we can
> stop making the sacrifices we had to make when

we had an avowed enemy that was a superpower.
Now we can look homeward even more and move
to set right what needs to be set right . . . for half
a century now, the American people have shoul-
dered the burden and paid taxes that were higher
than they would have been to support a defense
that was bigger than it would have been if imperial
communism had never existed. . . . Two years ago,
I began planning cuts in military spending that
reflected the changes of the new era. But now, this
year, with imperial communism gone, that process
can be accelerated. . . . The Secretary of Defense
recommended these cuts . . . By 1997 we will have
cut defense by 30 percent since I took office.

Bush and his secretary of defense, Dick Cheney, both knew
that there were still enemies and problems—this speech was
given a year after the Desert Storm war with Iraq—and yet
both of them pushed through major cuts in the defense budget
rather than seeking increases. Not so the second coming of a
Bush-Cheney team that more than doubled the defense budget
of Bush I. With the first President Bush, the peace dividend that
had been promised ever since the end of World War II seemed
at hand. The national security state that had become the norm
had lost its underpinnings, and America would return at long
last to a peacetime economy.

When I was a nine-year-old, at the time of V-E day, when
U.S. and Soviet troops hooked up victorious in Berlin, no one
in my neighborhood in the Bronx had predicted that with the
fall of Hitler we would be drawn into a new worldwide confrontation driven by a different ideology and committed for
the first time in U.S. history to what had all the markings of a

permanent war economy. This is not the place to argue whether the Cold War was necessary. But certainly after Gorbachev and the fall of the Soviet Union, there was no longer a justification for continuing this aberration of an America obsessed with war, as it has been after 9/11.

Obviously I knew of the threats posed by terrorists. Indeed, on May 22, 2001, four months before 9/11, I had warned in a *Los Angeles Times* column that Bush II was seriously underestimating the danger posed by bin Laden and his al Qaeda in Afghanistan, being more intent on that country controlling the drug trade than in its being used as a base from which to attack American targets. I also supported President Clinton's decision to try to take out bin Laden with cruise missile attacks, which Republicans in Congress condemned as a deliberate distraction from the all-important matter of the president's testimony in the Paula Jones case.

But it never occurred to me, or most other commentators on the issue, that what was needed was a doubling of the Defense Department budget to the height of Cold War levels. How the new enemy of a primitively armed stateless band of terrorists came to substitute for the Soviet Union as an enemy justifying an expansion of the military-industrial complex is the subject of this book. But I was naive to believe that those who profit from frightening us with images of the barbarians at the gates of our society would lack for such an enemy. Indeed, as I well knew from my own previous observations during the Cold War years, there never was a logically constructed correlation between the expenditure of military funds and a realistic appraisal of threats to our security. Threat inflation had long been the norm, and after the Cold War it became institutionalized.

In admitting his difficulty in defining the word "pornography," exasperated Supreme Court Justice Potter Stewart stated,

"I know it when I see it." That is how I feel about the use of the word in the title of this book. What it suggests to me is a vicarious experience that masks the real deal, substituting lurid and excitable imagery for an activity that is all too mundane and predictable. That pretty much sums up the antics of what President Dwight Eisenhower referred to in his Farewell Address, warning of the menace of the military-industrial complex. In the pages that follow, as you read of the gyrations of lobbyists and politicians eliciting billions for one weapons system or another in the name of fighting one enemy or another, see if you don't come to view it as a lap dance designed to hide the fact that all you are getting out of it is the opportunity to fork over ever larger amounts of your money. You might also wonder, "How did I let myself get seduced into this grimy and dangerous place just to get fleeced?" That is the basic question faced by our republic.

THE
PORNOGRAPHY
OF POWER

Chapter 1

THE GIFT OF 9/11

It cost between $400,000 and $500,000 for Osama bin Laden and his al Qaeda to pull off the 9/11 attacks, according to the authoritative estimate of the bipartisan 9/11 Commission appointed by President George W. Bush. But within days of the hijacking, Bush demanded fifty thousand times that amount—$20 billion—in emergency appropriations from Congress. By the time he leaves office, trillions of dollars will have been spent on what he dubbed the global war on terror (GWOT), with no end in sight and no logical connection between the money spent and the problem at hand. In this respect, Bush's reaction to 9/11 was all too typical.

The one thing they know how to do is spend money. For those who run the federal government, tragedy can be opportunity, and none so fortuitous than that represented by a frightful threat from abroad. Some wise political leaders have had the temerity to warn about the consequences of exploiting the foreign "engagements" cited in George Washington's Farewell Address. Others caution as to the dangers presented by the "military-industrial complex," that amalgam of the vast defense industry and U.S. military bureaucracy noted in Dwight Eisenhower's own parting presidential speech to the nation. But the norm is to begin to line the pockets of those who claim to defend us from the enemy at the gates with few questions asked about where the money is going.

It proved to be too good an opportunity for George W. Bush to pass up. Although he had de-emphasized foreign policy in his campaign and seemed to embrace the "new world order" of his father, favoring trade and diplomacy over military intervention, the post-9/11 Bush quickly recast himself as a wartime leader, a "war president," as he put it. While he had campaigned as a fiscal conservative and had promised a more modest defense buildup than the Democratic Gore-Lieberman ticket, he suddenly turned on the spigot full blast for Pentagon spending.

In a matter of days, "W" was no longer his father's son. In the months to come, he and his vice president, who had been a prudent secretary of defense during the first Bush presidency, would reverse Bush I's course. Those who didn't come along, like Colin Powell, would be ignored or exiled. Instead of the veterans of his father's administration, such as Brent Scowcroft and James Baker, Bush the Younger suddenly would embrace a neoconservative cabal that had united, most of all, in their shared contempt for the moderate foreign policy of his own father.

The first President Bush, a genuine war hero like Washington and Eisenhower, governed as a man of peace wary of the dangers of militarism. Indeed, it was precisely his restrained response in the first Gulf War, and his refusal to use that conflagration as an excuse to ramp up the post–Cold War Pentagon budget, that left him vulnerable to criticism from more bellicose quarters.

Bush I, once smeared as ineffectively dovish by the military hawks who fixated on his prescient wisdom in stopping short of occupying Iraq, was denied the second term that his quick but measured reaction to Saddam's aggression might have earned. He had demonstrated the logic of a sincere multinational approach to the world's problems, and even though his then secretary of defense, Dick Cheney, publicly endorsed that policy, Cheney and others eventually would turn against the "realist" approach of Bush I and join the neocon believers in a unilateral Pax Americana in response to 9/11.

Bush II lacked his father's seasoning in the consequences of war, and it is possible that his response to the stark assault of 9/11 was more startled swagger than measured confrontation. "Bring 'em on" was for Bush more a matter of thoughtless rhetoric than the substance of a considered foreign policy. As opposed to his father, who had fought courageously in a war and then served in key foreign policy positions as ambassador to China, head of the CIA, and vice president, George W. came to office without any serious history of involvement with the world. He had barely traveled abroad—some wilder frat boy–type adventures in Mexico and a visit with his ambassador father in China, where he complained that the cultural revolution crimped his dating style—were, prior to his presidency, the high points of his engagement with an increasingly complex world.

But the shock, or a cynic might say the opportunity, of the 9/11 attacks changed all that. For the rest of his time in office, Bush surrendered his presidency to those who identified national security with a wildly expansive U.S. presence in the world. And for the military-industrial complex that Eisenhower had warned against, Bush's transformation represented an end to the menace of fiscal restraint and an enormous windfall of new money from the government in Washington.

During the ten years before 9/11, Bush I and Clinton had presided over a post–Cold War era in which military confrontation was defended as a last recourse to be undertaken only when diplomacy failed, and then only with significant international support.

For the hawks—a disparate group of defense executives with a product to sell, politicians seeking reelection, and Pax Americana neocon ideologues—it was the worst of times. Those who had come to identify their own fortunes and that of the nation with massive military spending had been cast into a sorrowful limbo. Without a well-armed enemy in sight, the rationale for their massive claim on public funds had critically eroded.

Then the clouds parted after the attacks of 9/11. Suddenly these defense hawks and profiteers saw their moment, and the world of danger that had so rewarded them previously was reborn. Given the opportunity of a new international scourge to be combated—this time not communism but terrorism—there was much work to be done, and they knew just who could do it.

But would the new President Bush rise to the occasion? The hawks had their concerns; the president had never been much interested in foreign policy, let alone in fundamentally altering the world, and Condoleezza Rice, his national security adviser, along with Powell, had at times uttered words of reason and caution. Powell was a particular problem, in that he spoke with the authority of a veteran of battles that should not have been fought, and he seemed to be another war hero turned peacenik determined to avoid unnecessary wars.

However, there were the others in the administration of this untutored president who acted after 9/11 as if they never had met a war, or more important, an increase in military spending, that they couldn't endorse. Donald Rumsfeld flirted with Pentagon reform but did a quick about-face after the attacks. Then there was Dick Cheney, who had changed quite a bit since his days in the first Bush administration.

Cheney had moved through the revolving door between government and defense contractor Halliburton, where he was CEO, and had grown much closer to the neoconservatives, even signing off, as did Rumsfeld, on their Project for the New American Century, a neocon manifesto for strengthening America's military. Cheney and Rumsfeld criticized Clinton for not spending enough on defense, even though Clinton had exceeded the budget inherited from Cheney himself when he was secretary of defense in the outgoing Bush I administration.

Other members of the Bush II administration who had signed on to PNAC were Cheney's chief of staff, I. Lewis "Scooter" Libby, and deputy secretary of defense Paul Wolfowitz, among others. The neocon ideologues cannot be faulted for being secretive in their designs. The plan, some might say fantasy, was to seize the opportunity to beef up the military might of the world's only superpower, "to shape a new century favorable to American principles and interests," as was clearly laid out in the PNAC's founding statement written in 1997.

Suddenly, after 9/11, they had an unimagined opportunity to implement their vision, and they were not about to waste it. Old war plans were dusted off and historic grievances revisited, beginning with Iraq. The key neocon ideologues, with Wolfowitz as their most powerfully placed member, long had their sights set on overthrowing Saddam Hussein in Iraq, one of the goals of PNAC, and the lobbying for that position was soon fierce and persistent, as Richard Clarke and others on the opposing side in the Bush administration have documented.

In his memoir *Against All Enemies*, Clarke recalled his first formal attempt to brief key players in the Bush administration on the al Qaeda threat, in April 2001: "We need to put pressure on both the Taliban and al Qaeda," Clarke warned. But Paul Wolfowitz was not buying it. He "fidgeted and scowled" and when asked by Steve Hadley what was wrong, he replied, "Well, I just don't understand why we are beginning by talking about this one man, bin Laden." Clarke replied, "We are talking about a network of terrorist organizations called al Qaeda, that happens to be led by bin Laden, and we are talking about that network because it and it alone poses an immediate and serious threat to the United States." Wolfowitz answered, "Well, there are others that do as well, at least as much. Iraqi terrorism, for example." Clarke replied, "I am unaware of any Iraqi-sponsored terrorism directed at the United States, Paul, since 1993, and I think FBI and CIA concur in that judgment, right, John?" Clarke pointed at CIA deputy director John McLaughlin, who replied, "Yes, that is right, Dick. We have no evidence of any active Iraqi terrorist threat against the U.S." At which point, Wolfowitz turned to Clarke and said, "You give bin Laden too much credit. He could not do all these things like the 1993 attack on New York, not without a state sponsor. Just because FBI and CIA have failed to find linkages does not mean they don't exist."

Clarke wrote, "I could hardly believe it but Wolfowitz was actually spouting the totally discredited Laurie Mylroie theory that Iraq was behind the 1993 truck bomb at the World Trade Center, a theory that had been investigated for years and found to be totally untrue." Unfortunately, Wolfowitz's absurd view would carry the day with the president.

After 9/11, Bush came to buy into the neocon argument for overthrowing Saddam Hussein, despite having criticized Clinton's military intervention in Haiti as misguided "nation-building." But while there was disagreement in the administration as to where and when to intervene militarily in response to 9/11, there was broad agreement about the need to build up the Pentagon. In that endeavor, they found a chorus of support among the defense industry lobbyists and their congressional allies, who knew well how to seize an opportunity for more profits when it presented itself.

As dust from the debris was yet settling on the disasters of the World Trade Center and Pentagon, the White House, still woefully unclear as to the perpetrators and purposes of the attack, gave defense hawks what they wanted. The president drafted a request to Congress for that immediate allocation of $20 billion, chump change in the federal budget, but it set the tone for how the administration would now respond to the suddenly acknowledged threat of terrorism.

The amount, in terms of the spending that was to come, was very small—rivaling merely a decade's worth of U.S. humanitarian assistance to the rest of the world. However, such opportunity cost comparisons are rarely deemed relevant when it comes to the military budget. Unlike penny-pinching discussions concerning the cost of social programs, when the military is the subject it is difficult to get politicians or the media even to acknowledge the distinction between a million and a billion, let alone the trillion that the totally irrelevant Iraq war came to cost as part of the president's war on terror. But that first of a series of rising military budget requests set the basic tone for a new era of incredible waste. For the Pentagon, big money was once again in play.

With the stroke of a letter to the Speaker of the House requesting that multibillion-dollar down payment on this war, the president managed to fulfill the twin purposes of the national security budget—such a misnomer—by both rewarding his financial supporters in the defense industry and politically exploiting the concerns of a frightened nation. The sigh of relief among those whose livelihoods depend on maintaining the largest military machine at a cost approximating the combined expenditures of all other world nations, friend and foe, was palpable.

With the sudden demise of the Soviet Union a decade earlier, the military-industrial complex had lost its reason for being. The enemy in the Cold War was no more, but the real purpose of the bloated military budget, profit and jobs, persisted. And for those who stood to profit, the tragedy of 9/11 came to be viewed as a gift that would never stop giving. Communism may have come and gone as a bogeyman, but terrorism had been with us ever since a cave dweller first threatened his neighbors with a stone, and the war on terror, which Bush quickly branded this new offensive, was a splendid—and better yet, everlasting—surrogate for the Cold War.

The president's initial request for funding was presented as a stopgap measure, an early pittance of an installment on a spending binge that would in six years attain and then surpass the heights of Cold War budgets. Most amazing of all, it would end up financing many of the expensive weapons on the boards from the previous era that were obviously no longer justifiable in any sense except as a source of jobs and huge profit.

But who would notice in a nation traumatized by what the government and media propaganda machines were trumpeting from the first hours as a stunning attack that they shamelessly compared to the Japanese assault on Pearl Harbor? No matter that the ragtag band of religious fanatics who attacked this time did not possess an air force, other than the commercial one they commandeered from us on 9/11. This was war, and we needed to spend huge amounts of money to fight it. The surge of patriotism and the feeling of vulnerability following the attacks would leave few of any influence in Congress or the media daring to challenge this expenditure, or the doubling of the defense budget over the next decade.

Most of that new money was earmarked not for homeland security but rather for military expeditions abroad, beginning the most rapid peacetime buildup in American history. The result was the Pentagon budget for fiscal 2008 reaching a staggering $625 billion. Even after accounting for inflation, that leaves the Defense Department budget for the war on terror larger than at any time since the end of World War II, including the years covering the Korean and Vietnam wars as well as the Reagan buildup in the 1980s. And that is just for the Defense Department. Virtually every cabinet level department, including the newly created Department of Homeland Security, managed to get a piece of the war on terror budget.

What came to be known as "homeland security funding" was allocated to almost every government agency, and by the 2008 budget year, that slush fund had grown to $57.8 billion, with the largest share, $46.4 billion, allocated to the Homeland Security Department itself, created after 9/11. This of course proved a boon to the fortunes of the military-industrial complex. When all defense and security appropriations are combined, Winslow Wheeler of the Center for Defense Information and an expert on military spending estimates conservatively that the 2008 national security budget totals $878 billion.

No matter that the enemy precipitating this deluge of dollars was not a new Soviet-type empire with ten thousand nuclear weapons and a four-million-man army but rather a small band of terrorist thugs, a few of whom attacked us with pepper spray, Mace, and inexpensive knives of the Swiss Army and Leatherman varieties. No, this was an opportunity to resurrect a defense industry producing the most sophisticated weapons that had next to nothing to do with defeating terrorism but which comprised the totems of the religion of militarism: sleek and enormously expensive objects to be worshipped for their aura of power rather than their ability to smite one's enemies, real or imagined.

As with other religions among America's megachurches, the militarist sect fulfills the need for pseudospiritual purpose and commercial avarice, its god an amalgam of pious patriot and righteous banker who views greed as a virtue. For the next seven years, George W. preached this gospel, and a devoted and eager flock of defense contractors rewarded him with contributions. Homage to the military-industrial complex, where profiteering and the national interest are inextricably intertwined, provided Bush with a sense of eternal order in the wake of the chaos of 9/11.

"Yesterday, evil and despicable acts of terror were perpetrated against our fellow citizens. Our way of life, indeed our very freedom, came under attack," the president wrote in his September 12 letter to the Speaker of the House of Representatives. He knew very little about the attacks, but he knew that spending money, lots of it, would reassure the public:

> I ask the Congress to immediately pass and send to me the enclosed request for $20,000,000,000 in FY [fiscal year] 2001 emergency appropriations to provide resources to address the terrorist attacks on the United States that occurred on September 11, 2001, and the consequences of such attacks. Passing this supplemental appropriations bill without delay will send a powerful signal of unity to our fellow Americans and to the world. If additional resources are necessary, I will forward another request for additional funding.

Of course, the president already had access to enormous sums in the existing budget to allocate immediately, but his insistent demand for fresh money set the tone for the wildly excessive post-9/11 budgets to come. The initial $20 billion would quickly grow to a hundred billion, then a trillion, to fight this new "global war on terrorism," or "terror" as it came to be referred to in the president's speeches— "GWOT" in budget language throughout the federal government. The use of the word "war" was essential to justifying massive military spending to combat an enemy that had succeeded not with an army or sophisticated weaponry but only because of security system lapses that would require relatively minor expenditures to fix.

Getting the FBI, CIA, and Customs to communicate with each other about suspected terrorists would likely have prevented the lead hijackers from entering the country. Since fifteen of the "muscle" guys carried perfectly legal Saudi passports and were issued visas in that country, demanding accountability from the Saudi regime we had consistently coddled would have helped. Having more than the minuscule force of thirty-three air marshals who were on active duty prior to 9/11, and requiring safe cockpit doors, which the airplane manufacturers failed to build, also would have diminished the odds for the terrorists.

It was obvious, even in the first weeks after 9/11, that the problem was not a lack of money but rather a meager attention span. There had been official disregard from the White House to the clearly telegraphed intentions of bin Laden to attack inside the United States. Condoleezza Rice said as much April 8, 2004, at the 9/11 Commission hearing when she testified that the president's top secret daily briefing memo given to Bush on August 6, 2001, was titled "Bin Laden Determined to Strike Inside the U.S." As Bob Woodward and Dan Eggen wrote on May 18, 2002, in the *Washington Post*, the memo "was primarily focused on recounting al Qaeda's past efforts to attack and infiltrate the United States, senior administration officials said. The document . . . underscored that Osama bin Laden and his followers hoped to 'bring the fight to America,' in part as retaliation for U.S. missile strikes on al Qaeda camps in Afghanistan in 1998, according to knowledgeable sources."

Getting your national security adviser to pay attention to a blinking red warning light should have been corrected with a stiff reprimand from the president rather than by quickly throwing billions of taxpayer dollars at a vague target after the fact. But of course the president also deserved a reprimand, having systematically ignored warnings from the Clinton administration that an attack was coming. Unfortunately, prior to 9/11, the focus of this Bush administration had been on the drug war and not on terrorism at all. In one startling example of that, the Bush administration funneled $43 million in U.S. aid, to be distributed by an arm of the United Nations, to Taliban-controlled Afghanistan. Secretary of State Colin Powell announced the gift on May 17, 2001, specifically mentioning opium crop suppression as the rationale and assuring that the United States would "continue to look for ways to provide more assistance for Afghans."

Less than three months later, the U.S. assistant secretary of state for South Asia, Christina B. Rocca, met with Abdul Salam Zaeef, the Taliban ambassador to Pakistan, in Islamabad. According to the Associated Press, Rocca announced that, "[i]n recognition of the Taliban's elimination of opium, the Bush administration is giving $1.5 million to the United Nations Drug Control Program to finance crop substitution." This friendly meeting, which the Taliban's Zaeef called "very successful," took place on August 2, 2001—four days before Bush received his now infamous briefing on the imminent threat from al

Qaeda agents directed from Afghanistan who were already in sleeper cells in the United States, armed with explosives. The terror threat had just not been as important as the war on drugs.

But 9/11 changed all that. An administration that had been slow to respond to threats of danger became quick to request billions of dollars for the military establishment, as if this could have prevented the crisis. This strategy cleverly served the dual purpose of deflecting the public's attention from the administration's security lapses while leading Americans to believe that spending billions would make them safer. In the confusion following 9/11, that tactic, irrational as it obviously was, worked wonderfully for the president's previously sagging poll numbers.

The largest share of the first $20 billion post-9/11 appropriation, $7.4 billion, would be sent to the Department of Defense for "crisis and recovery operations and national security responsibilities," even though no one had yet figured out what weapons had been used to hijack the planes, let alone the nature of the enemy that had directed the attacks. What was clearly known was that the attacks were low-tech and familiar—airplane hijacking was after all not unheard of—and their use as destructive missiles had previously been planned by relatives of 9/11 mastermind Khalid Sheikh Mohammed. In addition, there was ample warning that such a tactic should be anticipated in the future.

Nothing about this attack suggested the involvement of a sophisticated military arsenal or even a state player, but the response, as evidenced by the invasion of Iraq, was to act as if the "evil empire" envisioned by Reagan had risen again, even though Iraq had no connection to 9/11. The United States proceeded to go to war not against the enemy that existed but rather the one desired by the military-industrial complex.

Money earmarked for the GWOT only represents part of the bonanza of 9/11 reaped by the defense industry, as the rest of the Defense Department budget grew dramatically—even though most of that increase was devoted to weapons that were relics from Cold War planning. Despite the fact that the collapse of the Soviet empire totally undermined the case for a new generation of planes, there was an enormous capital infusion into building stealth fighter planes designed to evade sophisticated radar systems in the Soviet Union that, like that superpower, no longer existed. Funding in the billions also was granted for a new generation of nuclear weapons that could never realistically be used to take out terrorists who specialize in finding cover among innocent civilians.

Consider the stunning example of Lockheed Martin's F-22 Raptor fighter at nearly $360 million a pop, with its stealth cover and elaborate electronics designed to counter threatened leaps in Soviet war-fighting capability that had evaporated with the end of the Cold War. The Center for Defense Information published an article (originally written for the *Los Angeles Times*) August 18, 2005, by Lawrence J. Korb, an assistant secretary of defense in the Reagan administration, in which he wrote that the F-22 Raptor "is the most unnecessary weapon system being built by the Pentagon. In fact, Defense Secretary Donald H. Rumsfeld tried to do away with it in the summer of 2002 but backed off when his Air Force secretary threatened to resign over the issue. It was originally designed to achieve air superiority over Soviet fighter jets, which will never be built."

The only thing good to say about this plane is that the Pentagon is only planning to buy around $65 billion worth, which is considerably less than the $300 billion price tag for the F-35 Joint Strike Fighter. That aircraft is also manufactured by Lockheed Martin, the nation's top defense contractor, and the one that doles out the most in campaign contributions. Whatever the value of these planes, why should 9/11 be cited by their proponents as justification for their purchase? As Korb points out, "The performance of the current generation of Air Force fighters in Afghanistan and Iraq makes it clear that the Air Force already has the capability to achieve air superiority against any enemies. The Taliban, al Qaeda, and Iraqi insurgents do not have jet fighters for the Raptor to conquer."

On September 9, 2001, two days before the al Qaeda attacks, Knight Ridder/Tribune Business News carried a report on the strenuous efforts of Lockheed to reverse congressional cuts in the F-22 fighter jet program. With profit and jobs at stake, lobbyists for the corporations, suppliers, and labor unions involved in the plane's production were scurrying around Capitol Hill under Lockheed's direction. It was not an easy sell, since the proposed plane no longer enjoyed even the most remote claim to military purpose, and according to the Knight Ridder article, in "what critics say is a classic example of the 'military-industrial complex' at work," the lobbying centered more on jobs than on national security.

Two days later, that all changed. Even though the F-22 had no conceivable role in preventing future hijackings of civilian planes or any other imagined terrorist tactic, the stealth plane and every other weapons system rendered obsolete with the end of the Cold War were suddenly repackaged as antiterrorist weapons. The most ludicrous example of the new antiterrorist mission created for the F-22 was the use of the plane to fly over Florida to protect the launch of space shuttles, presumably from an alien air force capable of shooting down older F-16 planes that might have been assigned to the task. The point is that the existing fighter fleet was more than adequate to handle any intrusion by a more mundane invader of Florida's skies.

The problem with the F-16 is not that it is out of date. On the contrary, the plane has been very successfully modernized over the years and is a fighter much in demand by nations throughout the world. So much so that Lockheed had to ramp up production to meet orders from Turkey, Greece, South Korea, and India. At the end of 2007, Lockheed had unfilled orders for 116 F-16s, with more coming in.

Air Force pilots from Netherlands, which has 213 of the planes, to Israel, with 200, favor the nimble F-16 as a plane of choice. "It has just incredible staying power" as a sales item, according to Lockheed's CFO Bruce L. Tanner. But that is just the problem. Why should the U.S. government invest upward of $300 billion to develop and purchase the F-35 or $65 billion on the F-22 when the F-16 is in most regards a better plane? There are 4,500 F-16s buzzing around the world, and not one has ever been defeated in any air battle.

But the stealthier F-22 was not the only high-tech wonder left purposeless with the end of the Cold War. The B-2 stealth bomber was designed to penetrate Soviet air defenses to destroy anyone or anything of value that had survived the initial retaliatory strike of our enormous nuclear-armed missile fleet. Of course, the bombers were redundant because by the time they arrived, if even a minority of the missiles had worked, there would be precious little left to destroy. Building a fleet of stealth bombers at more than $1.2 billion apiece was patently absurd.

Still, as long as the Cold War had endured, proponents of the B-2, led by primary contractor Northrop Grumman, were successful in making the case for the plane's development. What terrible timing for the company that the Cold War was ending when the plane made its first flight test on July 17, 1989. There were immediate technical problems with the plane—it lost much of its stealth cover in the rain, among other performance issues—but the clear problem for its continued development in the next years was that it had no military purpose. Indeed, Senator William Cohen of Maine, the ranking Republican on the Senate Armed Services Committee and later secretary of defense under Clinton, predicted in 1989 that, "[t]he B-2 won't make it." He instead called for money to be spent on rapid deployment forces better suited to a post–Cold War world.

However, the plane, as these weapons systems do, managed to retain some funding despite a lack of utility. Matters did look gloomy when Bush I, in his January 1992 State of the Union speech, announced that the B-2 fleet, once envisioned as totaling 135 aircraft, would be cut back to a mere twenty. Then came the war on terror, and, amazingly, a use was found for a stealth bomber designed to avoid super-sophisticated defense systems that neither the Taliban regime in Afghanistan nor Saddam Hussein's in Iraq possessed.

But don't let those facts get in the way of a good photo op. There was Vice President Dick Cheney, photographed in the belly of a B-2 bomber parked at Missouri's Whiteman Air Force Base on October 27, 2006, taking credit for this boondoggle: "I was proud, as secretary of defense, to be involved with the B-2 program during its early years," he said, insisting that he was vindicated by the plane's usefulness in the war on terror:

> To carry on in this fight, we need to project force across great distances, to hit targets with precision, and to move and maneuver without the enemy being able to track us. And that's exactly what we're able to do with the stealth technology of the B-2 bomber. Within weeks of September 11, 2001, B-2s were taking off from Whiteman, flying dozens of hours, refueling in flight, dropping

precision-guided, satellite-based ammunition on
Taliban and al Qaeda targets.

They were not precise enough, however, to have actually hit
any of the top leadership of the Taliban or al Qaeda, a function
better served by special forces already on the ground, as well
as planes already in the vicinity. Then there were those cruise
missiles, similar to those that Clinton had ordered fired into al
Qaeda base camps before 9/11, to dismal effect.

"The B-2 was critical, as well, to the liberation of Iraq and
the removal of Saddam Hussein," Cheney continued to an audience of military personnel and journalists, who apparently
never questioned that dubious statement. "On missions from
Whiteman and forward operating locations, B-2s flew more
than forty sorties and delivered hundreds of munitions against
enemy targets, helping take down a brutal dictatorship. These
aircraft remain essential to the continuing fight against terror,"
Cheney concluded. He never was asked by his media consort
to explain what stealth technology had to do with combating
insurgents, who could not have hit one of the bombers used in
World War II.

The stealth planes, the B-2s and F-22s, were but two of the
weapons designed to combat the Soviets that suddenly had been
orphaned by the loss of that enemy and now were adapted to
the new cause of antiterrorism. With the demise of the Soviet
navy, which was never much of a threat to U.S. fleets, it became
wasteful to construct new Virginia-class attack submarines at
a cost of about $2.5 billion apiece; but what the heck, it's only
money, and each of the service branches needs its new toys.
Who cares that the terrorists lack submarines for the U.S. Navy
to battle deep in the ocean, for which the Virginia-class submarine was designed?

For the Marine Corps, there is Boeing's V-22 Osprey tilt rotor aircraft that combines the vertical takeoff and landing of a helicopter with the flight pattern of a fixed-wing plane to ferry marines about. Twenty-five years in the making, these planes have crashed several times, killing their crews, and production always has been many billions of dollars over budget. A performance need was never proven, even in the old Cold War days. Dick Cheney tried to deep-six the Osprey when he was secretary of defense back in 1991, but Congress overruled him, and the plane continues to this day as a program expected to cost $55 billion, with an additional $20 billion already spent.

The spending spree that followed 9/11 was uncontrollable, but the question is, was it worth it? Did the expenditure of trillions of additional taxpayer dollars, including the long-run costs of the Iraq occupation, in addition to the more than $354 billion a year that already was being spent on the Pentagon before 9/11, have anything to do with preventing another such attack? Did it improve U.S. security?

Steve Kosiak of the Center for Strategic and Budgetary Assessments explained the dynamics of post-9/11 defense funding: "Both the administration and the armed services have incentive to put things in the [budget] requests for GWOT funding, whether it is related to war or not. It sounds better politically; it has that emergency ring to it. If you can attach something to a bill that deals with troop pay and armor, it will have smoother sailing."

Since President Bush cut taxes rather than raise them, the escalating costs of his war, including the interest on the money borrowed to pay for it, will be borne by taxpayers well into the future. And the trillions wasted on a swollen military budget, barely noticed at the time, will be the source of much soul-searching as we raise taxes and cut needed programs, military as well as domestic, in order to service a debt that never should have been incurred.

It was defense business as usual except with a multiplier effect provided by the war on terror. The money wasted was greater after 9/11, but the problem was endemic to the system that had developed during the Cold War. Ironically, one man who grasped this disconnect between spending and security was Secretary of Defense Donald Rumsfeld.

Chapter 2

RUMMY, WE HARDLY KNEW YE

Imagine it as the opening scene of a movie: Interior, Pentagon auditorium, camera pans the stage filled with uniformed military officers, interspersed with top civilian executives, behind Defense Secretary Donald Rumsfeld. The secretary seems quite stern as he sounds a dark warning to the hundreds of Pentagon managers assembled in the rows before him about the war they must wage against an implacable enemy, and win. The very survival of our nation is at stake:

> The topic today is an adversary that poses a threat, a serious threat, to the security of the United States of America. This adversary is one of the world's last bastions of central planning. It governs by dictating five-year plans. From a single capital, it attempts to impose its demands across time zones, continents, oceans and beyond. With brutal consistency, it stifles free thought and crushes new ideas. It disrupts the defense of

the United States and places the lives of men and women in uniform at risk.

Perhaps this adversary sounds like the former Soviet Union, but that enemy is gone; our foes are more subtle and implacable today. You may think I'm describing one of the last decrepit dictators of the world. But their day, too, is almost past, and they cannot match the strength and size of this adversary. The adversary is closer to home: It's the Pentagon bureaucracy.

This was Rumsfeld playing secretary of defense instead of secretary of war. He had been in his position for only eight months, but he knew there was a problem, and he wanted it fixed. He went on to decry the waste of hard-earned taxpayers' money: "An average American family works an entire year to generate $6,000 in income taxes. Here we spill many times that amount every hour by duplication and by inattention." He could have said every nanosecond and still have been vastly minimizing Pentagon waste on military programs that are poorly defined and in many cases not even properly accounted for, as he conceded: "Our financial systems are decades old. According to some estimates, we cannot track $2.3 trillion in transactions. We cannot share information from floor to floor in this building because it's stored on dozens of technological systems that are inaccessible or incompatible."

The speech echoed themes of Pentagon reform that Rumsfeld had announced soon after his appointment by Bush, but in this rendition, he was particularly devastating in his exposure of systematic waste. Even the media and public, not to mention Congress, which only occasionally and always halfheartedly monitors how taxpayers' dollars are spent on national defense, might have been shocked into action. But nothing of the sort happened. This historically exceptional anti-Pentagon tirade by an incumbent secretary of defense was totally ignored—because it was delivered by Rumsfeld on the tenth day of the ninth month of the year 2001, the day before what has become known simply as 9/11.

Before that day, bringing the military budget under control was possible. Indeed, given that the Cold War had ended a decade earlier, military reform and a peace dividend for taxpayers seemed an obvious imperative. As Rumsfeld put it, "We must change for a simple reason—the world has—and we have not yet changed sufficiently. The clearest and most important transformation is from a bipolar Cold War world where threats were visible and predictable, to one in which they arise from multiple sources, most of which are difficult to anticipate, and many of which are impossible even to know today."

Less than twenty-four hours later, Rumsfeld was at work in the Pentagon when he heard the sounds of a thunderous explosion as American Airlines flight 77 came crashing into his building complex. From that moment on, Rumsfeld's Pentagon reform project would be forgotten, and a new Cold War–style crusade, this time to rid the world of terrorism rather than communism, was under way in earnest.

The tough speech he gave just the day before, now a fading memory, honestly reflected the nation's security needs, offering heretical—and quickly forgotten—advice on how to give taxpayers the best bang for their buck. The occasion of Rumsfeld's speech that day was the kickoff of the Defense Department's Acquisition and Logistics Excellence Week. Rumsfeld began by first acknowledging E. C. "Pete" Aldridge Jr., undersecretary of defense for acquisition, technology, and logistics, a title that made him a very important man in the Pentagon. That's the guy who has to sign off before the checks are sent to buy all of the hundreds of billions of dollars worth of stuff—weapons, services, and personnel—that everyone else in the building wants and that Congress has agreed to pay for.

Aldridge was by then a sixty-three-year-old veteran of life in the military-industrial complex, having swung often through the revolving door between the Pentagon and the defense contractors they finance. Rumsfeld had made a point of hiring those with corporate experience, and Aldridge had it; he had been president of McDonnell Douglas Electronic Systems and had held other defense-related executive positions as well as posts in the government, including secretary of the Air Force.

Indeed, two years after his appointment under Rumsfeld, Aldridge resigned from the Defense Department to become a director of Lockheed Martin. Seven months later, President Bush appointed him to head the commission on space exploration to make recommendations on the future of NASA, despite the fact that Lockheed was one of the space agency's biggest contractors. Not unexpectedly, Aldridge's committee recommended privatizing NASA, and given the rapidly rotating door between the private and governmental sectors, one wonders whether the designation of the employer of record even matters. The defense industry is a quasi-socialist institution in every way except the distribution of profit. The taxpayers pay, and fellows like Aldridge profit, no matter who is cutting the check.

I don't know what Aldridge thought of his boss's remarks back on September 10, as Rumsfeld went on about cutting waste; Rumsfeld conceded that most in the audience would think they had heard it all before and didn't expect things to change, but it doesn't matter what Aldridge thought, or just how serious Rumsfeld was in making his heartfelt pitch for reform. After the events of the next day, when the Pentagon and World Trade Center buildings were attacked with civilian planes flown by terrorist hijackers, no one was strategizing about the prudent use of the public's money. Not then, and not for the remainder of the Bush presidency, in which the war on terror in effect came to obliterate reasoned discussion about the best way to budget for the nation's security.

Seven weeks after Rumsfeld's speech, the Pentagon, authorized by Aldridge, awarded a team led by Lockheed Martin a contract for what would become a $300 billion project to construct the F-35 Joint Strike Fighter, a multiservice futuristic combat plane. Yes, the same Lockheed Martin where Aldridge would become a director upon leaving the Pentagon less than two years later.

There is no free lunch. According to CorpWatch.org, "During the calendar year 2000, Lockheed Martin spent more than $9.8 million lobbying members of Congress and the Clinton administration, more than double the $4.2 million the company spent during 1999." The F-35 project had been kicking around for seven years and since 1995 had been the subject of an intense competition among defense contractors to determine which company would get to build the aircraft. Lockheed beat out Boeing for the multiservice plane, and during the years of debate in Congress by advocates of the two companies, the emphasis was far more on where the planes would be built and which Congress members would win the most campaign contributions and jobs for their district than over what was best to defeat a likely enemy. Even after 9/11, when the attack came from an enemy without an air force other than the commercial one they commandeered, U.S. media coverage of the decision to build the plane remained far more focused on jobs and profits than defeating terrorists with their pocketknives.

Reporting on Lockheed's victory in securing the contract, the *New York Times* on October 27, 2001, stated:

> The decision was a blow to the losing bid-
> der, Boeing, the nation's second largest military
> contractor after Lockheed. Boeing was already
> facing 30,000 layoffs in its commercial aircraft
> division . . . Immediately after the announcement,
> Boeing's allies on Capitol Hill said they would offer
> legislation requiring that production on the jet be
> split between the two companies. They also vowed
> to push the Pentagon to increase its purchases of
> other Boeing aircraft, including cargo planes and
> refueling tankers, to mitigate the company's eco-
> nomic woes.

You would think we were talking about the plight of home-less people here, or the family farm that was about to be seized by marshals, as the *Times* went on to note that Lockheed also could make a case for need-based government financing: "De-spite Boeing's problems, Lockheed Martin needed the contract more, analysts said." That was because Lockheed manufactured the F-16 and F-22 fighter jets that were thought to be at the end of their production run.

So much for defeating bin Laden and his gang that had struck six weeks earlier; the story was about jobs and profit and securing congressional votes, as the *Times* reported: "With so much money and so many jobs at stake, lobbying by the com-panies and their Congressional patrons was intense. Both com-panies spent millions on marketing, advertising and campaign contributions in the past year."

While Aldridge, as undersecretary for defense for acquisitions, had decided in favor of Lockheed and later became a director of the company, it should not be assumed that he did not feel Boeing's pain. Aldridge had been the president of McDonnell Douglas, which in 1996 also was eliminated from the F-35 competition and was forced to merge with Boeing. And in the Pentagon, Aldridge had gone along with the advice of pro-Boeing Congress members who had pushed for a consolation prize: Pentagon funding for the Boeing air tanker and the C-17 cargo plane. So what that those planes were not deemed necessary by the Pentagon; heck, the General Accounting Office had raised major objections about Lockheed's F-35 only a week before Aldridge signed off on that plane. The undersecretary was just doing his part on behalf of his former—and future—private sector employers.

He unabashedly noted in his March 2003 resignation letter to the president that one of his goals in the job had been "to improve the health of the defense industrial base." It was a goal on which he proudly claimed he "made significant progress on accomplishing." Without question, that goal became much easier to meet after 9/11, and his enthusiasm was evident in a friendly letter he wrote three weeks after that tragedy to his pals in the defense industry. The letter, which began "Dear Industry Partners," was sent just days before the U.S. invasion of Afghanistan, and it presaged profitable times ahead. Making clear the symbiotic relationship between industry and military, it continued:

> In the wake of our nation's recent shift to war footing, I would like to take this opportunity to express my gratitude for the tremendous contributions your companies make to our nation's security. If past conflicts are any guide, your products will

prove just as indispensable to our success in the arduous task ahead as the superb young Americans who will operate and utilize them.

I would also like to stress, during this national emergency, the importance of the use of discretion in all the public statements, press releases, and communications made by your respective companies, and by your major suppliers. As we all know, even seemingly innocuous industrial information can reveal much about military activities and intentions to the trained intelligence collector. Statistical, production, contracting, and delivery information can convey a tremendous amount of information that hostile intelligence organizations might find relevant. . . . Thank you again for your hard work and contributions. . . . Together we will prevail.

The wording of Aldridge's letter suggested that, under the guise of national security, contracting details between the military and industry could be withheld from the scrutiny of the American people, their representatives in Congress, and the media—"trained intelligence collectors" of a special sort.

Aldridge's penchant for secrecy is a convenient ploy of a defense insider, and after 9/11, the use of "national security" as a cover for waste and inefficiency became an all too easy argument to make. Under Aldridge's watch, the corruption that Rumsfeld had decried was greater, and the accountability he had called for was eviscerated. Rumsfeld himself had become part of the problem he had promised to solve.

Indeed, on April 1, 2005, Rumsfeld was being quizzed under oath by investigators from the Pentagon inspector general's office, an independent auditing body that reports to Congress as well as to the defense secretary. The subject was the very controversial $30 billion-plus program to lease those midair fuel tankers from the Boeing Company that congressional supporters of Boeing had demanded as a consolation prize for the company's losing the F-35 fighter contract to Lockheed Martin.

In a rare instance of effective congressional oversight, a very diligent Senator John McCain had blown that boondoggle out of the water. John W. Warner of Virginia, the Republican chairman of the Senate Armed Services Committee and a former secretary of the Navy, termed the tanker scandal "the most significant defense procurement mismanagement in contemporary history." The chief Air Force procurement officer who arranged the contract went to federal prison, as did the chief financial officer of Boeing. The company's chief executive officer was forced to resign, as did the secretary of the Air Force, and Boeing paid a fine of $615 million.

The details of that scandal are discussed as a case study in Pentagon corruption in the next chapter. But I mention it here as a measure of how far short of his earlier goal of procurement reform Rumsfeld's Pentagon would fall. Aldridge had signed off on the tanker contract in one of his last acts in office before leaving for Lockheed, and Rumsfeld was being queried by the Pentagon's own inspector general as to what he knew of the tanker scam, as well as many others that had surfaced on his watch.

Rumsfeld's answer was enormously revealing with respect to his plunging expectations of Pentagon reform, as R. Jeffrey Smith reported in the *Washington Post* on June 20, 2006, after receiving the transcript of Rumsfeld's testimony—following a year's delay—under a Freedom of Information Act request. According to the *Post*: ". . . Rumsfeld cited poor memory, loose office procedures, and a general distraction with 'the wars' in Iraq and Afghanistan to explain why he was unsure how his department came to nearly squander $30 billion leasing several hundred new tanker aircraft that its own experts had decided were not needed."

In short, although the military budget had doubled under his leadership of the Pentagon, he was in no better position to account for the money spent than the other guys he had complained about in his September 2001 speech, those who preceded him as defense secretary and who couldn't account for the missing $2.3 trillion. Even less so, as Smith reported: "The issue is relevant because a series of reports, including others by the inspector general and by the Government Accountability Office, indicate that five years into the Bush administration, the department's system of buying new weapons is broken and dysfunctional."

The *Post* quoted from a report by Comptroller General of the United States David M. Walker that severely condemned the Department of Defense procurement practices: "DOD is simply not positioned to deliver high-quality products in a timely and cost-effective fashion." He noted also that the Pentagon has "a long-standing track record of over-promising and un-delivering with virtual impunity."

Walker's criticism was based on a study of fifty-two weapons systems with a whopping collective price tag of $850 billion. He concluded: "The all too-frequent result is that large and expensive programs are continually rebaselined, cut back or even scrapped after years of failing to achieve promised capability. A lot of it is because in the past, where there have been unacceptable outcomes, there hasn't been any accountability." Rumsfeld came in for criticism for this sorry state of affairs from Comptroller Walker, who said of the defense secretary that he "does not seem to be pushing" for a fundamental change in the system. Recall the quotes from Rumsfeld promising to reform the Pentagon; instead, the waste and corruption of unaccountable and pointless expenditures was exacerbated under his leadership, as revealed in the investigation of the tanker deal.

The question put to Rumsfeld by the inspector general's agents was whether his aides, particularly Aldridge, were accurate when they stated that Rumsfeld approved the tanker-leasing deal. Rumsfeld at first hedged: "I don't remember approving it, but I certainly don't remember not approving it, if you will," he said. When pressed by somewhat incredulous investigators if his subordinates had been deceptive in saying he supported the deal, Rumsfeld hemmed and hawed in the very bureaucratic cop-out style that he previously had condemned: "I may very well have said yes. I just don't remember. . . . I am not going to sit here and quibble over it." Smith noted: "He did say he remembered approving a gun for a tank in 1976 during his first time as defense secretary."

It was a sad concession for Rumsfeld, who had prided himself on bringing a can-do efficiency to all of his management assignments inside and outside of government. The excuse for his failing, and for so much that has gone wrong this decade, was, of course, "9/11 made me do it." Rumsfeld, who earlier had complained that Pentagon bureaucrats were indifferent to the waste of $6,000 that an average family paid in taxes, now defended his being ignorant of a deal that spent $30 billion for leased tankers the Pentagon had not officially requested. He had been preoccupied, he told the investigators, by "the global war on terror" and the "continuing difficulties" with the Taliban and al Qaeda. "My time basically in the department was focused on those things and certainly not on acquisitions or—or what have you," Rumsfeld said. "Basically I spend an overwhelming portion of my time with the combatant commanders and functioning as the link between the president . . . and the combatant commanders conducting the wars."

Rumsfeld was asked if he was concerned that the Pentagon had failed to follow its own procedures on the tanker deal, including conducting an Analysis of Alternatives, the comparative cost analysis of different options required by Defense Department regulations. Rumsfeld, who most prided himself on staying on top of details, said he wasn't, and noted, "You are way out of my league on all of this."

Ignorance as to the true cost of the administration's loudly proclaimed "war on terror" after 9/11 was not unique to Rumsfeld. It characterized the general response of an administration that had come into office promising fiscal restraint but quickly abandoned that pledge after 9/11. Nor were the Democrats in Congress much better, as they more or less had voted enthusiastically for the rapidly rising Pentagon budgets. What followed, as revealed in the case studies detailed in subsequent chapters, was a greed fest of unprecedented proportions. Hundreds of billions of taxpayer dollars were thrown at defense contractors with wild abandon, justified by incessant references to the global war on terror, as if it were the drug of choice at some wild orgy.

Chapter 3

THE FALCONS
COME HOME TO ROOST

The business of the military, particularly concerning the expenditure of huge sums of taxpayer money on weapons systems, is by design an opaque subject having more to do with bureaucratic prerogatives and corporate profits than the actual use of those weapons in waging war. There is little enthusiasm among those in the decision-making process for any measure of transparency, which would serve no one's interest except the taxpayers who foot the bill.

Each year, an intricate budget-allocation minuet—a dance of legislators, Pentagon officials, and corporate lobbyists—is conducted and largely ignored by the mass media, and therefore the public. This annual ritual matters a great deal in the division of spoils, and it is a process deliberately shrouded in mystery by its primary practitioners. Only through a rare window, and usually when scandal erupts, do outsiders catch a glimpse of the system's deep corruption. The Boeing air-refueling tanker scandal in the post-9/11 Congress provided just such a telling, if passing, glance.

As Congress set about addressing the president's request for additional funding ostensibly to meet the challenge of 9/11, it was all too convenient for legislators and lobbyists, the main players in the game of military spending, to recast their feeding at the public trough in the urgent language of antiterrorism. The president has demanded a blank check—and received one—every budget year since. National security spending more than doubled over the decade, and most of that outflow of money had nothing to do with a logical response to the 9/11 attacks. But in the emotional aftermath, it was rare for anyone to effectively challenge the new terms of debate, and thus little debate ensued.

Take the needs of one major defense contractor, the Boeing Company. As the nation's leading manufacturer of civilian aircraft, Boeing was in big trouble after 9/11 because of widespread anxieties about air travel. Congress recognized that commercial carriers were foundering and within two weeks after the attacks passed a $15 billion bailout to assist them. As Boeing faced problems such as reduced orders for its commercial jets, company lobbyists and government allies attempted a number of taxpayer-financed remedies. Among those potential solutions was a plan to persuade the Air Force to lease Boeing 767 commercial planes and modify them to serve as in-flight refuelers for long-range aircraft, or "gas stations in the sky," as neocon pundits Richard Perle and Thomas Donnelly approvingly called them in their *Wall Street Journal* column from August 14, 2003.

Whatever the value of repurposing these planes instead of relying on or upgrading the Air Force's available stock of refueling tankers, pre-9/11 efforts to interest the Pentagon in a similar scheme to purchase those Boeing planes had yielded only a negative response. Internal Pentagon reviews, as well as those from other branches of government, had concluded that the existing Air Force tanker fleet was performing adequately, and the president's budget submitted to Congress before 9/11 did not include provisions for purchasing or, as would later be advocated, leasing the Boeing planes. The deal was initially estimated to be worth about $20 billion, then $35 billion, and if fully funded it represented a potential $100 billion windfall for Boeing.

But prospects were bleak—before 9/11, that is. From September 12, 2001, onward, any objections that the 767 was a plane that the Pentagon had not asked for would be easily ignored. The end result of this myopia was what came to be known in inner circles as the Boeing Air Force tanker scandal, a wonderful mélange of hawkish ideology and corporate greed that exemplifies the modus operandi of the military-industrial complex. The scandal—hardly unique, although one of the most outrageous—is known to the public only because of the exposé instigated by Republican Senator John McCain.

As a Vietnam-era prisoner of war, McCain's commitment to the security of the nation could not be challenged easily, and thus his constant criticism of Pentagon waste has been particularly effective. The other side of this bizarre tale features neocon ideologue Richard Perle; a top Pentagon procurement officer who served time in federal prison, as did the CFO of Boeing; the then secretary of the Air Force, who resigned amidst the scandal; and the CEO of the Boeing Company, who was also forced to step down.

The scandal developed after 9/11, when the president and Congress had an opportunity to recast government defense spending to better guard against this new terrorist enemy. The president's request for $20 billion in the immediate aftermath of 9/11 would cover the short-run responses to rebuild and improve security, but what about the nation's overall military posture? After a decade of approving post–Cold War budgets more by rote than necessity, given the collapse of our prime enemy, our country's leaders now could reevaluate the nation's defense needs in light of the new urgency to combat international terrorism. But that is not what occurred.

As it happened, the president had been late in submitting the overall 2002 defense budget, and as a result, the weeks after 9/11 found Congress still actively grappling with the minutiae of appropriations for the Pentagon's pre-9/11 military spending requests. Then the spending frenzy began, and the setting was ripe for corruption. Winslow T. Wheeler, for thirty-one years a top staff member on national security issues for the U.S. Senate and General Accounting Office, wrote a biting essay in 2002 assessing Congress's defense budget shenanigans in response to 9/11. Wheeler's title says it all: "Mr. Smith Is Dead: No One Stands in the Way as Congress Laces Post-September 11 Defense Bills with Pork."

Wheeler circulated the essay under the pseudonym Spartacus, saluting the Roman slave and gladiator who led a slave insurrection in 73 BCE and was later killed in battle with Roman soldiers. Wheeler's fate at the hands of Senate Republicans was less severe; he merely lost his position with the Republican staff of the Senate Budget Committee when his identity as Spartacus became known. Just as he was nonpartisan in his choice of bosses, being the rare Senate staff member to work for both Democratic and Republican senators (Republican Nancy L. Kassebaum of Kansas and Democrat David Pryor of Arkansas), he was nonpartisan in his criticism.

Wheeler's point, well documented as only an insider who has mastered the deliberate mysteries of the congressional budget could do, was that nothing was done to alter the budget to respond to the new crisis, and everything was done to fine-tune the product in Congress members' time-honored tradition of assuaging key voter blocs and campaign contributors before all else. The urgent dangers brought to light by the 9/11 attacks presented new opportunities for these legislators that made their business as usual pork barreling seem so shocking. The "Mr. Smith" he referred to was the character played by Jimmy Stewart in the film classic *Mr. Smith Goes to Washington*; the title reflects Wheeler's disappointment that the one member of Congress who had come closest to playing that role in his opposition to pork, Senator John McCain, had dropped the ball just like his colleagues.

Despite the heartfelt urgency in the rhetoric about combating terrorism, with just about all of the items Congress approved, few of those expenditures had to do with making the country more secure. Take, for example, the military construction bill where, as Wheeler documents, money was suddenly added for items in congressional members' home districts or states:

> Altogether, Congress added about 120 new construction projects not requested by the president. Of these, just two were training facilities, and just one directly involved security. The balance of what was added constituted a hodgepodge of irrelevancies; they included plans for a new museum, a new chapel, gyms, warehouses, fire stations, water towers, land acquisition, daycare centers, National Guard armories (which Congress renamed "readiness centers") and much else.

Unsurprisingly, at $144 million, the biggest beneficiary of this distribution was California, the home state of Democratic Senator Dianne Feinstein, then chair of the Senate's Military

Construction Subcommittee, which crafted its own $10.5 billion measure. Feinstein, upon submitting the military appropriations construction bill on September 26, 2001, proclaimed:

> Given the events of the past few weeks and the events that we expect to unfold over the coming weeks and months, this bill could not be more timely. . . . We have a duty to provide better for the members of our military and their families, especially at a time when the president has ordered them to "be ready" for war.

As Wheeler commented:

> The hypocrisy of these comments is rather stunning: having laden the bill with $144 million in pork for her own home state and doing virtually nothing elsewhere in the bill to aid the war against terror, chairwoman Feinstein was pretending that her handiwork was both relevant and urgent. . . . Senator Feinstein was hardly alone, and she was hardly the most offensive.

Exhibiting his flair for warranted bipartisan scorn, Wheeler took on Republican Senator John McCain, the "Mr. Smith" he pronounced dead, for being the senator who had been most visible in the past in challenging congressional pork but seemed ineffectual in stopping the post-9/11 budget grab. Wheeler was particularly upset that McCain, after a strong public showing of contempt for one of the more egregious swindles of the moment, a gift of $35 billion in the sweetheart tanker leasing deal with Boeing, had seemed to throw in the towel.

But in this instance, Wheeler would come to be proven uncharacteristically wrong. Perhaps due in part to that scathing criticism from Wheeler in 2002, McCain launched a Mr. Smith–style crusade over the next two years that led to the felony convictions of the Pentagon's top procurement officer and Boeing's CFO, the resignation of Boeing's CEO, and the cancellation of the Pentagon contract. As a result of McCain's success in enforcing the public release of internal Pentagon and Boeing memos, the public was provided with a rare glimpse into the defense contractor's ability to coerce the Air Force and the media to make the case for one of the greatest military spending boondoggles ever.

Among those who tried to sell the plane to the public were a former admiral on Boeing's payroll and neocon Richard Perle, an author of the *Wall Street Journal* article castigating critics of the plane-lease program without revealing that his venture capital company had received a $20 million investment from Boeing. This time, the real-life Mr. Smith lived up to his billing.

On November 19, 2004, three years after Congress approved the plane lease scam, McCain rose on the floor of the U.S. Senate to lay out the case against the Boeing–Air Force deal that he and his staff had painstakingly uncovered:

> Nearly three years ago, behind closed doors, the Appropriations Committee slipped a $30 billion rider in the fiscal year 2002 defense appropriations bill. This rider authorized the Air Force to lease from Boeing up to one hundred 767s for use as aerial refueling tankers. Before the rider appeared in the bill, Air Force leadership never came to the authorizing committees about this issue. In fact, tankers have never come up in either the

President's budget or the Defense Department's unfunded priority list. The Air Force's tanker lease program was born of a virgin birth.

The rider was, in fact, the result of an aggressive behind-the-scenes effort by the Boeing Corporation with considerable assistance from senior Air Force procurement official Darleen Druyun and others. After the President signed the bill into law, the Air Force embarked on negotiating with Boeing a lease that would have cost the taxpayers around $6 billion more than an outright purchase of these aircraft would have.

The Darleen Druyun to whom McCain referred was the top procurement officer for the Air Force who had pled guilty to corruption for granting this and other huge contracts to Boeing while negotiating for jobs with the company for herself and members of her family. Indeed, at the time she went to federal prison in October 2004 to serve her sentence, she was a $250,000-a-year vice president at Boeing. But previously, for more than a decade in the Pentagon, Druyun had exercised often undisputed power over the expenditure of hundreds of billions in U.S. taxpayer dollars, and the question raised by McCain in his speech was how she could have committed this crime alone:

> I am going to tell a story that has not, as I said, reached its end. But it has uncovered the very strong likelihood, because of the confession by Ms. Druyun in federal court when she pled guilty, that there could be many billions of dollars of the taxpayers' money that were wasted, criminally treated,

and misused because of the decisions made by Ms. Druyun. The question is, how could Ms. Druyun have done all this by herself? Did she have accomplices or was the system in the Pentagon so broken that one individual could make contracting decisions which entailed tens of billions of dollars, and in this case may have cost the taxpayers of America millions and even billions of dollars as well?

Druyun's guilty plea agreement cited specific examples of favoring Boeing, including agreeing to a higher price for Boeing aerial refueling tankers than she thought appropriate; giving proprietary pricing data to Boeing as a "parting gift" and to ingratiate herself with her future employer; sharing proprietary bidding data from Boeing's aerial tanker competitor, Airbus, a subsidiary of EADS, the large European aerospace corporation; awarding $100 million to Boeing in 2002 as part of a NATO early warning system contract, when the award could have been for less, because her daughter worked there; settling with Boeing for $412 million in a contract dispute when her future son-in-law was seeking employment there; and choosing Boeing over four competitors in 2001 for a $4 billion contract to upgrade C-130 aircraft because the firm had hired her son-in-law. Ms. Druyun conceded in the court papers that Boeing likely would not have won the contract otherwise.

Family ties proved useful to Druyun, as revealed in e-mails between her daughter, Heather McKee, who worked in human resources for Boeing, and the company's chief financial officer, Michael M. Sears. As Reuters reporter Andrea Shalal-Esa wrote in April 2004, when Druyun pled guilty, McKee e-mailed Sears on September 5, 2002, about her mother's preferred job requirements: "The perfect offer would be a COO [chief operating officer]-like position," McKee told Sears, passing on her mother's detailed description of her preferred job. Mother and daughter had a talk about the position during a visit in St. Louis, where McKee worked, and "It is the tanker lease that prevents her from talking to you right away," McKee told Sears. According to the Reuters report, "McKee closed by saying of mom: 'She is very interested in talking to us. . . . She also mentioned that Boeing has her most admired quality: honest values.'" Aw, shucks. About six weeks later, Sears offered Druyun a job. She did not recuse herself from Boeing business until November of that year.

The conviction of Druyun, who also was fined $5,000, was followed by the conviction of Boeing's CFO, Sears, who was sentenced on February 18, 2005, to four months in prison, a $250,000 fine and two hundred hours of community service, and was forced out of his job. Boeing CEO Phil Condit resigned on December 1, 2003; the company was fined $615 million, and the contract for the tanker was frozen. The scandal rocked Boeing and led to investigations of other contracts with which Druyun was involved, along with heightened scrutiny of the company's other dealings with the government.

The reverberations were still being felt almost two years after McCain's Senate address and prompted an unusually candid speech by Douglas G. Bain, Boeing's senior vice president and general counsel, at a Boeing Leadership Conference in Orlando, Florida, on January 5, 2006, a transcript of which was printed in the *Seattle Times* January 31, 2006. The mood was somber as Bain began his remarks with a bit of gallows humor: "Good morning. As I walked up here, I think I heard [Boeing chairman and CEO] Jim McNerney mutter 'Here comes Dr. Death.'" Bain's remarks provided a rare glimpse into the defense business beyond corporate PR as he stated,

I want to talk about these scandals not so much
from the perspective of how we have tried to argue
them or spin them, but from the perspective of the
prosecutors and what they have told us. The recur-
ring message we have gotten from the prosecutors
and frankly everybody else we deal with is one of
shock and surprise.

What follows is a searing indictment by Boeing's general
counsel listing examples of ethical corners cut, crimes committed, and moral indifference and/or complicity all the way to
the top. The tanker deal was only one of the scandals involving
Boeing, but Bain spelled it out with chilling clarity:

> On October 17, 2002, Mike Sears [then chief
> financial officer of Boeing] flew in a company air-
> plane down here to Orlando and met with Darleen
> Druyun [then chief acquisitions officer for the Air
> Force] and offered her a job.
>
> The question everyone keeps asking is, why? The
> rules on dealing with government employees are not
> hard. In fact, during the meeting Darleen told him,
> "I have not recused myself from Boeing business."
>
> As best we can figure out, Darleen told Mike
> in Orlando that she had just received a handshake
> offer, which she had accepted, from Lockheed
> Martin. It's my personal belief that Mike then went
> into a sales mode. He not only wanted to make
> sure that he got Darleen, he wanted to make sure
> that Lockheed Martin did not.
>
> The next day, Mike sent an e-mail that said, "I
> had a 'non-meeting' with Darleen Druyun."

If this were all we were facing, we might have been able to deal with it better. But there were a lot of other events that came out. It turned out, in August 2002, Mike had had Darleen come to Chicago, and even though the R word was never used, the prosecutors say, "this looks like a recruitment meeting." So maybe the October 17 conversation was not a one-off.

During the month of September, there was a string of e-mails between Mike and Darleen's daughter, who was employed as an HR person [for Boeing] in St. Louis. The e-mails clearly are negotiations for Darleen coming to work for us.

Again, if this is all we were dealing with, we might have had a different issue. However, in the year 2000, Darleen sent a copy of the résumé for her future son-in-law to Mike, asking for his assistance in getting him a job. Mike merely sent on the résumé, did not ask for anything to be done. But the people who received it assumed Mike was going to say "Make it happen"—and they did. A few months later, this had worked; Darleen sent the résumé of her daughter to Mike. Same thing happened. Mike sent the résumé along, and the people made it happen.

All this stuff came together when Darleen was sentenced, and she said "I might have favored Boeing in awarding contracts" because of the favors Boeing had done for her in hiring the son-in-law and the daughter.

So, the cultural questions: How come nobody said to Mike, "what in the hell do you mean by a

non-meeting?" How come in the year 2000 nobody said, "Should we really be hiring the relatives
of our chief procurement officer for the largest
customer we have on the defense side?"

The federal court had already answered that question, and
Druyun's $250,000-a-year job in Boeing's missile defense pro-
gram led to a $5,000 fine and a stint as prisoner number 47614
serving nine months in federal prison. Boeing CFO Michael M.
Sears became prisoner number 70040. He also forfeited $5 mil-
lion in compensation when his employer forced him out.

The reverberations from the Boeing scandal hit the company
hard. As Bain conceded, "there are some within the prosecutors' offices that believe that Boeing is rotten to the core. They
talk to us about pervasive misconduct and they describe it in
geographic terms of spanning Cape Canaveral to Huntington
Beach, to Orlando, to St. Louis to Chicago." He then cited
details, such as the U.S. attorney in Los Angeles "looking at
indicting Boeing for violations of the Economic Espionage Act,
the Procurement Integrity Act, the False Claims Act, and the
major Frauds Act."

Bain also listed similar investigations by U.S. attorneys across
the country and warned that nothing less than the future of the
company was at stake, even suggesting, "We can lose our security
clearances." All this, of course, was occurring under a Justice Department in a Bush administration with which Boeing had close
ties. Yet, said Bain, "When we first met with the Department of
Justice to see if we could resolve this, it's their view Boeing's actions have tainted the EELV contract [the space rocket program],
the NASA 19-pack contract [a 2002 contract for up to 19 Delta
II rocket launches], and 27 Darleen-Druyun-related contracts.
Their estimate of damage is $5 billion to $10 billion."

This is the same Darleen Druyun who had received nine awards for distinguished service in her years with the Pentagon, including two presidential awards, one Secretary of Defense citation, and a Secretary of Defense Meritorious Civilian Civil Service Award. Her official biography in the Air Force archives lauds her for "initiatives [that] have yielded more than $20 billion in savings to the Air Force." True, that was before the unpleasantness.

At least in that speech to top management by the company's general counsel, Boeing was prepared to face up to some of its major problems, but not so the people in the Pentagon who had hired Darleen Druyun, and in Senator McCain's view had to know of, and therefore condone, her activities. While there were resignations at the Pentagon, the story was largely reported, as is typically the case, with Druyun cast as the bad apple, perhaps not sufficiently supervised by higher-ups but not emblematic of a more profound corruption within the government's military procurement program.

McCain wasn't buying it. As he pointed out at Senate hearings and in speeches, the e-mail trail produced by his prodding and that of Republican Armed Services Committee Chairman John Warner clearly shows that Druyun did not act alone within the Pentagon. Indeed, her lobbying for the tanker plane had the support of Air Force Secretary James G. Roche, a former Navy captain who had spent seventeen years as a vice president of defense contractor Northrop Grumman, which was hustling contracts with the Pentagon before Bush appointed this corporate fox to guard the henhouse as secretary of the Air Force.

Roche, who was an advocate for the Boeing tanker lease program, stepped down from his Air Force post January 20, 2005. That was shortly before the Pentagon's then inspector general, Joseph E. Schmitz, found the Air Force secretary to have violated two military ethics rules when he urged his former employer, Northrop Grumman, in 2003 to hire the brother of Office of Management and Budget associate director Robin Cleveland at a time when Roche was trying to get the OMB—which vehemently opposed the tanker-leasing deal—to support it.

Senator John McCain made public many e-mails related to the tanker deal, including this exchange between Cleveland, who asks Roche for the favor, then his response to her showing he forwarded the résumé to his friend at Northrop Grumman (NG), and an e-mail from Cleveland to her brother. Roche and Cleveland both mention the tanker in their e-mails. The brother was not hired by the defense contractor.

From: Robin Cleveland

To: Jim Roche

Sent: 9 May 2003 1549

Subj: Peter Cleveland resume and cover letter/Import compliance attorney (DC) position-02 1495

Jim: This is my brother's stuff. I would appreciate anything you can do to help with NG. He is an incredibly hard working, disciplined guy—worked full time with two little kids putting himself through law school at night. I would be grateful. Thanks very much, Robin.

From: Jim Roche

To: Robin Cleveland

Sent: 9 May 2003 1712

Subj: Peter Cleveland Resume & Cover letter attached for export

Be well. Smile. Give tankers now (Oops, did I say that? My new deal is terrific.) :) Jim.

Dr. James G. Roche,

Secretary of the Air Force.

From: Jim Roche

To: Stephen Dyslas Northrop Grumman

Sent: 9 May 2003 1620

Subj: Peter Cleveland Resume and cover letter attached for export/import compliance attorney (DC) position-021495

Steve: I know this guy. He is good. His sister (Robin) is in charge of defense and intel at OMB. We used to work together in Senate staff. If Peter Cleveland looks good to you, PLS add my endorsement. Be well. I've let Rummy con me one more time! Army! Best to Alice.

Jim.

From: Robin Cleveland

To: Peter Cleveland

Sent: 15 May 2003 1913

Subj: Re: Interview at NG

Great hope it works before the tanker leasing issue gets fouled up.

The e-mails between Roche and his colleagues at the Pentagon are as sordid as they are revealing of the routinely intimate connection between top Pentagon officials and the corporate honchos with whom they do business. Just to taste the flavor, consider an e-mail from Roche's special assistant William C. Bodie on April 25, 2002, describing an encounter he had with Rudy de Leon, Boeing's D.C.–based senior vice president of government relations. De Leon had previously held several positions in the Defense Department, including deputy secretary of defense, and had been undersecretary of the Air Force. Bodie e-mailed Roche that he saw de Leon at the Kennedy Center and "politely asked the Great White Arab Tribe of the North [a

Pentagon insider phrase for Boeing] to unleash their falcons on our behalf for once." He said he also lined up defense analyst Loren Thompson to comment to a reporter on the need for the tanker, and that Vago Muradian, editor of *Defense News* and *Air Force Times*, "is also standing by."

What was going on here was a joint propaganda campaign being waged by top Pentagon officials in tight coordination with the chief Washington representative of the Boeing Company to spur Congress to appropriate money for a tanker program that the Pentagon had not even officially requested. But in the hysteria after 9/11 it would turn out to be an easy pitch, as the "falcons"—meaning those pundits and others claiming to be experts on preserving the nation's security—swooped down on their congressional prey. Here's one possible strategy that falcons could employ: Find an admiral, write something up for him, and get your buddies over at *Defense News* to run it, implying that this is merely an expression of sincere concern by an experienced military veteran for the vital defense of the nation.

As McCain, who read the e-mail to his Senate colleagues, described it:

> Among the falcons that Boeing "unleashed" was an op-ed that subsequently appeared in Vago Muradian's *Defense News*. This piece, which strongly endorsed Boeing's tanker lease, was supposedly written by former commander in chief for U.S. Pacific Fleet, Admiral Archie Clemins. However, Admiral Clemins has admitted, and Boeing's emails reflect, that it was in fact ghost-written and placed by Boeing.

Clemins's article ran in the influential *Defense News* in March 2003, as Congress was considering the tanker deal, but eight months later, after Clemins's ties to Boeing were revealed, the publication carried a disclaimer entitled "Full Disclosure" which conceded:

> What we didn't know at the time [of publication] was that Clemins did not write the piece. Nor did he think on his own to write it. Nor, for that matter, did he even think to send it to *Navy Times*, a sister publication, without prompting. In truth, a Boeing representative came up with the idea, asked Clemins to write it, and provided a writer to help get the job done. Boeing also suggested where he ought to send it and provided him the e-mail address.

The magazine went on to note that Clemins insists he was not paid to write the article, "But he acknowledged that prior to writing the article, he had done some paid consulting work for Boeing, and that he has since developed a more formal consulting arrangement with the company."

How cozy. And Admiral Clemins was hardly the only falcon unleashed by Boeing. However, the admiral-turned-consultant denies that he did it for the money and insists that he believes in the words that were written for him. He probably speaks the truth, for it is not all that difficult to talk oneself into believing that the nation's security will be well served by spending taxpayer dollars on a program that will profit your corporate sponsor.

In that regard, I assume that Richard Perle, probably the most famous of the falcons, also came to genuinely believe in the "gas stations in the sky." Perle and his fellow American Enterprise Institute defense hawk Thomas Donnelly likely wrote their own piece with that title, and one can even accept that they believed in the argument that they made for the Boeing tanker lease program, excoriating those in the government who dared to challenge the expenditure of $30 billion. They took particular umbrage with the General Accounting Office finding that "the urgency of [tanker] replacement is unclear."

How dare they oppose this defense expenditure when, thanks to 9/11, Perle and his colleague could invoke the ever-useful war on terror:

> It takes a special government green-eyeshade mentality to miss the urgency of the tanker requirement. Government calculations almost always are based on straight-line projections that the future will be just like the past; but big events like the war on terrorism simply cannot be quantified in this way. And if Sept. 11 does not reasonably generate new "requirements," nothing does.

Now why in the world would you need a hundred gas-filled tankers flying around to thwart airplane hijackers? That might be an obvious rejoinder if by "war on terrorism" Perle was referring to what actually happened on 9/11. But he wasn't, and instead, the argument of his piece rested on the usefulness of air refueling in the Iraq war, an event with no logical connection to 9/11 and one that Perle did much to inspire.

In the column, Perle describes the magnificent usefulness of midair refueling to the Iraq "shock and awe" campaign, without seeming to note that it was conducted not by the Boeing 767s that Perle was pushing to be leased, but rather executed quite effectively by the existing KC-135 tanker aircraft that the Air Force already owned. In short, the success of the Iraq invasion was confirmation that the existing tanker fleet was more than adequate to the task and that there certainly was no urgent need to replace it with the leased Boeing planes. Unless, that is—and here's the rub with Perle—one plans on additional, simultaneous Iraq-style invasions.

That Perle does indeed have in mind such extensive use of air power in wars throughout the world is clearly telegraphed in his column when he notes that the tankers are merely a stopgap measure until we can develop more Cold War stealth B-2s capable of flying to distant targets without requiring midair refueling: "We would be wise to invest more in long-range bombers—more B-2s, for example—since the ability to operate globally on short notice will be vital to winning the war on terror. In the meantime, however, let's make the most we have of the fleet we have by supporting it properly."

The B-2, perhaps the greatest of Air Force boondoggles, is an enormously expensive plane outfitted with a cover designed to provide stealth protection sufficient to evade radar so sophisticated that the Soviets never possessed it. As was noted earlier in describing Cheney's celebration of the B-2, it is an absurd weapon for defeating terrorists. However, it is an excellent plane if one is planning to extend U.S. power as part of a "Pax Americana" plan of superpower domination, which was precisely Perle's intention.

Chapter 4

"DO YOU KNOW THERE'S A FEE?"

They call him the Prince of Darkness, and for his many critics, Richard Perle has become the symbol of all that went wrong with American foreign policy in the aftermath of 9/11. It is Perle who emerges from the now substantial collection of memoirs and other insider accounts as a—if not *the*—central figure driving the original neoconservative group around the Project for the New American Century that long had pushed for the overthrow of Saddam Hussein. After 9/11, he was a key player within Donald Rumsfeld's Pentagon doing just that. Not to take anything away from the other true believers who formed the inner circle of the neocon cabal, such as William Kristol and Paul Wolfowitz, but Perle certainly has been a star player at this game as long as anyone.

I first met Perle when he was a brash young foreign policy aide to Senator Henry "Scoop" Jackson, the hawkish Democrat from the state of Washington who commonly was referred to as the "senator from Boeing" for his unwavering support for the huge aerospace company that then was headquartered in his home state. Jackson was not a man of many ideas, and his predictable support of any weapons system that could possibly benefit Boeing, and hence produce campaign contributions and jobs back home, seemed to be at the core of his ideology—until he met Perle. This new aide was already a hardened ideologue whose dark view of the undifferentiated and unchanging scourge of international communism soon became the senator's own. I had spent weeks with Scoop for a profile I wrote about him for *Esquire* magazine in 1975, and I noted at the time that, "Though Scoop sounds scary on the intensification of the Cold War into the eighties, he seems mild in comparison" to Perle. At the time I had assumed that, as opposed to the senator, Perle was a sincere hawk determined to combat communism not to increase corporate profits, but to save the world.

When one reads the statement of the Project for the New American Century, which Perle did much to inspire, the tone is exactly the same as I heard from the man back then: There was evil afoot in the world, and only America could be trusted to combat it. In the post–Cold War PNAC statement, he is even loath to give up the expectation (or is it hope?) that China, if not a revived Russia, might still be expected to perform as the center of a revitalized evil empire. That view was convenient for those directly in the employ of the arms industry, but as for Perle, I assumed that his motives remained, as in the old days, purely ideological, if wrong.

Call me naive; it just seemed too simplistic to think that all pro-military hawks are in it for the money. True, for the better part of the past century, foreign policy had been directed by Wall Street lawyers, recycled defense executives, and others, like Dick Cheney, who made a huge bundle while claiming to be primarily interested in the security of their country. But we long have been propagandized into believing that the pecuniary interest of war profiteers is not their main driving force. I tend to fall for that line because sending people to kill and be killed in a war that you don't believe in just sounds too cynical, and most of these folks present quite effectively as morally concerned citizens.

It was perhaps for that reason that even I was shocked when news first broke in 2003 that Trireme, a start-up company listing Perle as a principal partner, had received a $20 million investment from the Boeing Company. Yes, Scoop's old mainstay. And this risky investment had been made before Perle wrote the *Wall Street Journal* column cited in Chapter 3 denouncing Pentagon budget watchers for daring to object to the leasing of tankers that Boeing was trying to palm off in a deal worth billions to the company. That Perle neglected to tell his *Journal* editors of this potential conflict of interest raises troubling ethical questions. As it happens, it was not an isolated incident.

On April 17, 1983, Jeff Gerth reported in the *New York Times* that Perle, then assistant secretary of defense for international security policy in the Reagan administration, had recommended that the Army consider buying Israeli-manufactured mortars under a deal that was potentially worth hundreds of millions of dollars to a company that a year earlier had paid him $50,000 for "consulting." Perle said that he received payment the same month he joined the administration, March 1981, for "promoting mortar sales" before he joined the government. He said he had told Army Secretary John Marsh that he had worked for the Israeli company he recommended. The Army retained the contract with the then current British supplier, despite a letter from Perle to Marsh complaining that the British supplier was being protected from competition.

Gerth reported that Perle admitted having other consulting contracts: "He said that he had several other military consulting contracts in early 1981, including a $5,000 agreement with TRW, a major military contractor. The company's files show Mr. Perle signed a one-year agreement with TRW on April 1, 1981, eight days after he began work at the Pentagon. The company said it canceled the contract as of June 30, and on June 25, paid Mr. Perle the $5,000."

A *New York Times* editorial four days later pointed out that while Perle did not break a law, what he did "falls beneath the standard set by other government officials who disqualify themselves from matters involving former clients or employers." It noted that under the Pentagon's practice of granting contracts without competition, "influence becomes a precious commodity. No wonder companies are willing to pay enormous fees to people who are in a position to further their aims."

How true that would be for Perle over the years to come. After leaving the Reagan administration in 1987, he moved quickly through the revolving door and soon was a director on more than a dozen corporate boards. That is not so unusual, except that Perle kept one foot in government while the other was stomping through the private sector. I know the physiology here is strained, but the image captures Perle's hyperkinetic shenanigans perfectly. As *Washington Post* reporter David S. Hilzenrath wrote on May 24, 2004, in an article headlined "The Ultimate Insider":

> On one level, Perle's business career is like those of many former Washington officials who used the expertise and contacts gained in government to carve niches in the corporate world. But more than most, Perle also has maintained an active public policy role. . . . Unlike many who pass through Washington's revolving door, Perle for seventeen years managed to keep one foot in the

government as a member of the Defense Policy Board, which offers advice on key issues to the secretary of defense.

Perle was appointed to that board in 1987 and served until 2004; he was board chair from 2001 to 2003, when he stepped down from that position, though not from the board, for yet another alleged conflict of interest. The problem with having two feet planted in different worlds is that straddling can become very awkward. Consider Perle and China.

In his policy capacity, Perle frequently sounded the alarm against China, as he had years before when the Chicoms were expected to invade Seattle if we didn't defeat their surrogates in Vietnam. The Project for the New American Century statement that Perle helped write also made much of the prospect of a revival of Red China as an enemy. Yet in his private sector work, Perle served as a paid consultant to Global Crossing Limited, which was trying to secure U.S. government approval for its sale to a Chinese-Singaporean venture, a transaction resisted by the Defense Department and the FBI. The problem was that Global Crossing's worldwide fiber optic network, which was used by the federal government, would be transferred to Chinese ownership with the sale.

Perle's predicament, aside from the fact that *New York Times* reporter Stephen Labaton exposed it on March 21, 2003, was that as chair of the Defense Policy Board, he was in a class called "special government employees" who are barred under federal ethics rules from using their positions for private gain. Perle told Labaton that he was merely advising Global Crossing on how to get approval for their business deal and not lobbying Pentagon officials on behalf of the company. Global Crossing, then on the verge of bankruptcy, was paying Perle $725,000, of which

$600,000 depended on the U.S. government approving the deal, which was made when the Chinese partner withdrew.

The Defense Policy Board is not technically a government agency, and its thirty or so members, who include former high-ranking government officials, military officers, and academics, are not paid. However, they are in a position to benefit financially. Fortunately for Perle, the Defense Department inspector general investigating his business activities determined in November 2003 that he worked for the Pentagon so infrequently—a mere eight days a year—that he therefore did not have to meet the stringent code of conduct rules.

The *New York Times* Global Crossing story was published less than two weeks after a *New Yorker* article by investigative reporter Seymour Hersh detailed a lunch meeting arranged by Saudi businessman Adnan Khashoggi between Perle and a wealthy Saudi industrialist named Harb Saleh al-Zuhair. In the story, released on the Web March 9 and in the print issue dated March 17, 2003, Hersh wrote that according to the two Saudi men, whom he interviewed, the main agenda was "to pave the way for Zuhair to put together a group of ten Saudi businessmen who would invest ten million dollars each in Trireme." Hersh noted that

> Trireme's main business, according to a two-page letter that one of its representatives sent to Khashoggi last November [2002], is to invest in companies dealing in technology, goods, and services that are of value to homeland security and defense. The letter argued that the fear of terrorism would increase the demand for such products in Europe and in countries like Saudi Arabia and Singapore. . . . The letter said that forty-five mil-

lion dollars had already been raised, including twenty million dollars from Boeing; the purpose, clearly, was to attract more investors, such as Khashoggi and Zuhair.

Hersh wrote the two men "told me that they understood that one of Trireme's objectives was to seek the help of influential Saudis to win homeland-security contracts with the Saudi royal family for the businesses it financed. The profits for such contracts could be substantial."

According to Hersh, the letter sent to Khashoggi pointed out that three Trireme management group members were then serving on the Defense Policy Board, "and one of Trireme's principals, Richard Perle, is chairman of that board." The letter added that two other Trireme associates, former Secretary of State Henry Kissinger and Gerald Hillman, who ran Trireme's New York office, also were on the defense board. Hersh pointed out, however, that Kissinger was only part of the advisory group and not part of the management team.

Hersh noted Zuhair had his own agenda in agreeing to the meeting with Perle. He was a Saudi born in Iraq and wanted to help avert the pending war. He had been to Baghdad and "wanted to share his views on war and peace with someone who had influence with the Bush Administration." He got his wish: The luncheon with Perle was held in Marseille on January 3, 2003. Before that meeting, Hillman sent Khashoggi two memorandums suggesting more than a dozen or so terms to be met for the United States to not go to war and to "ascertain that Iraq is sincere in its desire to surrender."

Conditions included an admission by Saddam that "Iraq has developed, and possesses, weapons of mass destruction," followed by his exile from the country along with his sons and some ministers of his government. Hersh reported that Zuhair thought the terms "absurd"; Khashoggi "thought they were amusing, and almost silly." When interviewed by Hersh, Hillman insisted that Perle had nothing to do with writing the letters, although "he never said one word" when Hillman sent them to him. But Hillman conceded that he did have assistance; "he had drafted the memorandums with the help of his daughter, a college student." Imagine her surprise when the memos made their way into the Saudi-owned newspaper *Al Hayat* and the Beirut newspaper *Al Safir*, portraying the memos as American documents, with Perle representing the United States in the American-Saudi meetings. The memos thus caused something of a stir.

Of course, allowing one "political" agenda item—peace in Iraq—at the lunch meeting would then allow Perle to deny a strictly moneymaking goal. Hersh reported that Perle told him Trireme "'was never mentioned and never discussed . . . it just would never have occurred to me to discuss investments, given the circumstances.' Perle added that one of the Saudis had information that Saddam was ready to surrender. 'His message was a plea to negotiate with Saddam.'" Zuhair had told Hersh that one of Hillman's requests of him was to set up a meeting with the Saudi chief of intelligence in Washington, D.C. That meeting might have been aimed at benefiting Trireme more than the peace process.

The conflicts seemed dubious: Here were Perle's own company, standing to profit from a war of which he was one of the most vociferous advocates; Perle's positions in Trireme and as chair of the defense policy board, which he advised about matters that might affect his company; and flaunting the relationships between other defense board members and Trireme in order to attract investors.

The fallout was great, the damage was done, and Perle

stepped down as defense board chair on March 27, 2003, though not from the board itself until the following year. A bit testy about the Hersh story, Perle denied any conflict and told CNN's Wolf Blitzer the day the story broke: "Sy Hersh is the closest thing American journalism has to a terrorist, frankly."

Hersh, a meticulous and excellent journalist who has won the Pulitzer Prize and broken dozens of major stories, beginning with his exposé of the My Lai massacre by U.S. troops in Vietnam, doesn't need any defending here. But although Hersh once again got it right, this time in his treatment of Perle, the journalist's "terrorist" attack was hardly fatal. Indeed, despite—or because of—controversy, Perle had become something of a money machine in demand by others wanting a piece of the take.

As Stephen Labaton wrote in the *New York Times*: "Mr. Perle, who as chairman of the Defense Policy Board has been a leading advocate of the United States' invasion of Iraq, spoke on Wednesday [March 19, 2003] in a conference call sponsored by Goldman Sachs, in which he advised participants on possible investment opportunities arising from the war. The conference title was 'Implications of an Imminent War: Iraq Now, North Korea Next?'" Drat. The United States, with some careful diplomatic maneuvering, cooled down the North Korean crisis. Maybe Iran? No matter—war is good business for the war profiteer, wherever it occurs.

In another arrangement that raised conflict-of-interest questions, Perle was a paid consultant to Loral Space & Communications when it faced allegations by the U.S. government of leaking sensitive material on rocket launchers to the Chinese. Perle told the *New York Times* he was hired before being named to the defense board and did not lobby the government on behalf of Loral.

Perle was not above using his access to scoop up petty cash. A report by Ari Berman posted online July 31, 2003, in *The Nation* magazine detailed how, when he was chair of the defense board, Perle demanded payments for interviews in the $100 to $900 range from international media outlets. Seen to be an influential figure close to the president, secretary of defense, and other foreign policy decision-makers, Perle was in demand as a spokesperson on U.S. policy on Iraq, particularly leading into the war.

For example, a week after millions of antiwar protesters had marched throughout Europe before the U.S. invasion of Iraq, a European television station asked Perle, as chair of the Defense Policy Board, to talk about the United States' Iraq policy. He demanded a fee, Berman wrote, and the station agreed, violating its own policy of not paying for interviews. As Berman reported, Perle's pecuniary drive in this instance fit a pattern of behavior.

"We did pay Perle because of his position [in a] prominent advisorship to the Secretary of Defense," says a European correspondent who, like most journalists interviewed, requested anonymity because of network discomfort at publicly discussing payment policies.

Perle was not doing anything illegal as he told Berman. Although Perle would sometimes declare that he was appearing as a fellow of the American Enterprise Institute for Public Policy Research, foreign news organizations saw him in a more exalted role. As a Japanese news producer whose policy also prohibits paying for interviews explained: "When we break the rules, it's for heavy-hitting individuals like Richard Perle."

Berman noted that one correspondent asked a Perle assistant for an interview and was told: "Do you know there's a fee?" A "typical Perle appearance," Berman wrote, occurred on April 4, 2003, on a Canadian morning news show for which Perle was paid $900.

The host introduced Perle as a lead architect of Iraq policy and "one of the closest advisers of

Donald Rumsfeld and a member of the influential Defense Policy Board." In the interview, Perle described the war in Iraq as certain to be "a quick war by any standards" and asserted that "we will find weapons of mass destruction when the people who know where they are are free to talk to us." On May 29 he was invited back and was paid for discussing Bush's Middle East policy.

But Perle wasn't foolish enough to let a few measly dollars distract him from the big-time cash his day jobs supplied. As in the case of China, his public espousal of a very strong pro-Israel policy line stood at odds with his eagerness to do business with Arab governments that proclaim opposition to Israel's legitimacy. Perle conceded in the interview in the *Washington Post* that he had contacted ambassadors from Saudi Arabia and Kuwait in the 1990s for a company on whose board of directors he served and for which he was a sales consultant. "Was that a result of my influence?" he asked rhetorically, then answered, "Yeah, it was. It was a result of the fact that they, the people I went to, knew me so they took my phone call."

The *Washington Post* story exposed a number of such deals consummated after Perle left his full-time employment in the Pentagon in 1987. As assistant defense secretary for international security policy, Perle played an active role in relations with Turkey, and he was known to support increased military assistance to that country. After Perle left the Pentagon, FMC Corporation, a U.S. defense contractor eager to sell armed personnel carriers to Turkey, signed Perle up because, as the company's then chief executive told the *Washington Post*, Perle's "main asset to us was his relationship with the Turkish government." The former CEO, Robert H. Malott, said a U.S.

ambassador to Turkey told him the Turks regarded Perle "as a demigod."

The *Washington Post* story represents a rare look into the economic motivations that may be connected to the fervor that Perle and other extremely hawkish neoconservative intellectuals have demonstrated for a larger military to back a more aggressive U.S. presence in the world. If nothing else, their public political posture, as the Turkish ambassador indicated, translates into demigodlike influence in the marketplace as well. But it is not just Perle who has exploited his political role to advance his personal financial fortunes, as demonstrated by the Turkish connection with another major neocon, Douglas J. Feith, who also played a leading role in the Bush administration.

Feith attained much prominence during the run-up to the Iraq war when, as undersecretary of defense in Donald Rumsfeld's Pentagon, he headed the special intelligence unit that cherry-picked classified data to counter the consensus in the intelligence community that there was no urgent reason to move against Saddam Hussein's mythical weapons of mass destruction. Feith and Perle played a decisive role in crafting that fiction. But the alliance of Feith and Perle did not begin with the Iraq war; Feith worked for Perle in the Defense Department in the 1980s and the two had financial dealings at least since 1989, when Perle cut Feith into his dealings with Turkey.

The $1.1 billion FMC Corporation deal with Turkey to purchase 1,700 armored personnel carriers was finalized in 1989, and Perle modestly told the *Washington Post* that he hardly deserved the major credit since the deal was "essentially done." However, less modestly, he did take credit for the "occasions" when he talked about the deal with his "good friend," the Turkish Prime Minister Turgut Özal. Evidently at that same time, he also urged the Turks to establish a lobby operation in Washington, and they did so, making a deal with International Advisors, Inc., a company led by Feith.

Perle did not register as a lobbyist for Turkey but was paid $255,000 from Feith's firm from 1989 through the beginning of 1994 for consulting, according to the *Post*. While Perle was putting together the PNAC alliance for a more vigorous U.S. foreign policy that stressed a go-it-alone American role unencumbered by undue attention to the concerns of other, particularly Western European nations, he was being handsomely rewarded for helping extend Turkish influence over U.S. policy.

In 1996, Feith and Perle, along with fellow neocon David Wurmser, who later would join the State Department and become Mideast adviser to Vice President Dick Cheney, were among a team of eight who produced a paper on the future of Israel—from their perspective. The paper was titled "A Clean Break: A New Strategy for Securing the Realm." It was published by the Institute for Advanced Strategic and Political Studies, an Israeli think tank, for the incoming government of Benjamin Netanyahu.

Among other things, it suggested, seven years before the Iraq invasion, that a new bright future for Israel should begin by throwing out Saddam Hussein from Iraq and installing a Hashemite monarchy in his place. The report said:

> Israel can shape its strategic environment, in cooperation with Turkey and Jordan, by weakening, containing, and even rolling back Syria. This effort can focus on removing Saddam Hussein from power in Iraq—an important Israeli strategic objective in its own right—as a means of foiling Syria's regional ambitions. Jordan has challenged Syria's regional ambitions recently by suggesting

the restoration of the Hashemites in Iraq. . . . Were the Hashemites to control Iraq, they could use their influence over Najf to help Israel wean the south Lebanese Shia away from Hizballah, Iran, and Syria. . . . Israel will not only contain its foes; it will transcend them.

As history has recorded, Perle, Feith, and Wurmser were among the most vociferous proponents of the Iraq war, which would accomplish that key goal of the "Clean Break" paper. Just two years after writing the report, the Project for the New American Century published, on January 26, 1998, a letter to President Clinton urging war against Iraq and the removal of Saddam Hussein. On what grounds? Saddam represented a "hazard" to "a significant portion of the world's supply of oil." Foreshadowing what eventually would happen, the letter called for the United States to go to war alone, attacked the United Nations, and said the U.S. should not be "crippled by a misguided insistence on unanimity in the U.N. Security Council." The letter was signed by many who would later lead the 2003 Iraq war, and ten of the eighteen signatories later joined the Bush administration.

Perle spoke with authority in March 2001 when he told the Senate Foreign Relations Committee,

Does Saddam [Hussein] now have weapons of mass destruction? Sure he does. We know he has chemical weapons. We know he has biological weapons. . . . How far he has gone on the nuclear-weapons side I do not think we really know. My guess is it is further than we think. It's always further than we think, because we limit ourselves, as

we think about this, to what we're able to prove
and demonstrate, and, unless you believe that we
have uncovered everything, you have to assume
there is more than we're able to report. . . .

Perle spoke in his capacity as chair of the Defense Policy
Board, whose members are given top secret briefings, so the
committee members had no reason to believe Perle did not know
what he was talking about. Only five days after the September 11
attacks, he was quick to announce on CNN that Saddam Hussein was linked to Osama bin Laden. Asked if he believed the
United States should take action "against terrorists or people who
harbor terrorists, even if they are not necessarily associated" with
the 9/11 attacks, Perle replied: "Even if we cannot prove to the
standards that we enjoy in our own civil society that they were
involved. We do know, for example, that Saddam Hussein has ties
to Osama bin Laden. That can be documented."

Feith, as undersecretary of defense for policy, oversaw two
secretive operations at the Pentagon that provided "evidence" of
ties between Saddam Hussein and al Qaeda, which proved to be
fraudulent. While Feith continues to defend the integrity of his
work, the groups he led, Counter Terrorism Evaluation Group
and Office of Special Plans, earned the scorn of the Pentagon's
inspector general, who found Feith's office to have "developed,
produced, and then disseminated [to senior decision-makers]
alternative intelligence assessments on the Iraq-al Qaeda relationship, which included some conclusions that were inconsistent with
the consensus of the intelligence community." Former Secretary
of State Colin Powell called Feith's group the "Gestapo office."

Those years before Iraq, between the Reagan era and the
coming of George W. Bush to the White House, were very
profitable for Perle, even as his political campaign against what

he thought was the softness of the Clinton administration was in full sway. But his business connections sometimes proved very controversial and might have threatened his public persona had the media in general been as vigilant as was David S. Hilzenrath, the *Washington Post* reporter.

Among other items in his report, Hilzenrath dealt with the fifteen-year relationship between Perle and the British Morgan Crucible Co. PLC. It is instructive that Perle came to the attention of the company's top executives, who asked him to join their board after he spoke at a London conference hosted by an investment bank.

At Morgan Crucible, Perle was confronted with some legally tinged controversy when the U.S. subsidiary of the company, Morganite, Inc., in 2002 admitted to price-fixing and agreed to pay a $10 million criminal fine. Perle claimed to have no responsibility in the case, and speaking of the board on which he served, noted that it "conducted itself in an exemplary fashion." It is not difficult to accept that Perle was unaware of the company's illegal activity in the United States, since participation on a board of directors, while lucrative, is not always very demanding.

It is difficult to accept that that was the case with Perle's work on the board of Vikonics, Inc., which he joined in 1990. Remember that this was a mere three years after Perle left the Defense Department, and Vikonics is a company that sells security systems to the military. In addition to his board position, Perle also had a consulting deal with Vikonics that paid him a 7 percent commission on contracts he assisted in the company obtaining.

According to John L. Kaufman, who was the president of the company at that time, Perle's role was to spin the classic revolving door that connects the defense contractor to people still inside the Pentagon who could authorize purchases. As he told the *Washington Post*: "What he (Perle) really had done was help us with introductions to people who he knew . . . high-ranking people in the areas of government there and in the military."

By "there" Kaufman was referring to other potential government purchasers, citing his trip to Kuwait, where former defense official Perle was in high standing after the United States had saved the country from Saddam Hussein. In Kuwait, Kaufman recalled, "The minister of this or the secretary of that—no matter who it was, everyone wanted to meet him. I do believe that he did help us to gain contracts just by being there to help us."

No doubt, but what does it mean for a major player in the formulation of U.S. policy toward countries like Kuwait, both when Perle was at times in the government or in one of his frequent consulting roles, to actively parlay the contacts earned in that official capacity into profitable contracts? Does it not in the very least skew his perspective on the internal politics of Kuwait and the U.S. "interest" in that country?

In 1994, four years after Perle had joined the Vikonics board, the company could boast of securing a contract to provide a security system to the ministry of information in Kuwait, and business with that country soon flourished. Perle, when confronted by the *Washington Post* about his role in the sale, did not deny making a contribution, and even volunteered that he had telephoned Prince Bandar bin Sultan, the very high profile Saudi Arabian ambassador to the United States, concerning Vikonics: "I talked to Bandar and said I'm on the board of this company, and we make some very high quality security devices, and if there's a market for these in Saudi Arabia, we'd like to go talk to people who make those decisions. Same thing in Kuwait."

Prince Bandar bin Sultan is not just some guy you call to sell an alarm system for his house. This was one of the most influential representatives from the Arab world in Washington, D.C., attempting to shape U.S. policy toward the region. The first Gulf War was fought primarily to ensure the survival of the royal family in Saudi Arabia, which had many dealings with U.S. corporate interests, extending well into the Bush family.

The second Gulf War was fought, ostensibly, in response to the attack on the World Trade Center and the Pentagon, and fifteen of the nineteen hijackers came from Saudi Arabia. Not one came from Iraq. Yet in the hours after the attack, the Bush administration demonstrated concern for the safety of Saudi officials in Washington and expedited their hasty departure from the United States before they could be confronted and questioned about how the Saudi hijackers managed to obtain valid passports from the Saudi government to travel to the United States.

Meanwhile, in those same hours, the neocons, including Perle, in and around the Bush administration, were agitating to use 9/11 as the excuse for toppling Saudi Arabia's longtime enemy, Saddam Hussein.

Has Perle ever talked to the man he familiarly refers to as "Bandar" about how those fifteen Saudis managed to travel so easily from Saudi Arabia to this country and what connections they might have had back home that would explain their dastardly behavior? This is the most obviously important yet least examined aspect of the 9/11 attacks. Who were those guys who made the attacks possible, what motivated them, how were they financed, and what role did Saudi religious and political institutions have in making this happen?

Given Perle's position as chair of the Defense Policy Board at the time of these attacks, and his key role in advocating the U.S. response of attacking Iraq, surely some investigative agency or reporter might have been interested in finding out what the ever so closely connected Perle knew about the Saudi aspect of this tragedy. That they weren't, and that Perle's Saudi ties went largely unnoticed at the time, speaks volumes about our blind acceptance of the neocons' ethical protestations. Despite a profit stake in the exertion of U.S. military power, they insist they acted professionally, if hawkishly biased, when peddling political advice, whether in their government jobs or as pundits on the talk shows.

Washington Post reporter Hilzenrath shed light on other connections between Perle, defense contractors, and foreign governments, including his relationship with Raytheon Company, one of the largest U.S. defense contractors, back in what were evidently very lucrative years for Perle in the early 1990s. First, as Hilzenrath reported, Raytheon hired the American Enterprise Institute, where Perle was a fellow, to provide advice about business possibilities in Turkey. Perle "was one of the associates involved in that process," Raytheon declared in a statement. Okay, but what is the AEI, which presents itself as a community of scholarly experts who happen to take a strong pro-defense position, doing getting money from defense contractors and hawking influence in Turkey? Need you ask?

Significantly, Perle helped Raytheon sell Patriot missiles to Turkey in the early 1990s. The Center for Public Integrity, in a "Windfalls of War" company profile, pointed out that in June 1991, "the Defense Department awarded Raytheon a $346.3 million modification to an existing contract, which included funding for thirty-two Patriot missiles for Turkey under a foreign military sale."

Perle proved his true friendship to Turkey while in the Reagan administration Pentagon, when, in 1986, as *The Nation* magazine writer Jason Vest wrote in an article August 23, 2002,

Perle got credit for "closing a deal for a five-year Defense and Economic Cooperation Agreement with Turkey which the *Financial Times* characterized as 'something of a personal triumph' for Perle." Turkey became the third-largest recipient of U.S. military aid, after Israel and Egypt, and, Vest noted, "got a nice break on debts owed to the United States."

Meanwhile, the door keeps revolving. Focusing on Perle should not obscure the fact that his actions after emerging from the Reagan Pentagon were hardly far from the norm. As Hilzenrath reported in the *Washington Post*, while Perle was at FMC selling armored personnel carriers to Turkey, Edward C. Meyer, the former chief of staff of the Army, was a fellow director at FMC, and the two men served together on three additional boards. They do manage to scratch each other's backs, as the *Post* story noted: "An investment firm Meyer helped manage granted Perle stock options to run for a board seat. The options produced a profit of about $250,000 for Perle. At Perle's recommendation, Meyer was appointed to join him on another board."

When folks like Perle and Meyer offer their somber appraisals of the security concerns of the nation, is it in any way conceivable that they are not also thinking about how this might play out in current or future business dealings?

In what now seems like the distant past, there were scholars who more vigorously pursued ideas concerning the functioning of business and corporate elites. Indeed, one of the leaders in that effort, C. Wright Mills in his seminal work *The Power Elite*, published five years before Eisenhower's Farewell Address, described the power trio of the military, corporate, and political establishments.

One difficulty in attempting to define centers of power is that when they attain notoriety through such publicity, they often lose their usefulness as watering holes where the powerful are inclined to gather. One such center, maybe the one most often cited, was the Bilderberg Conference, a secretive, invitation-only get-together of European and North American power brokers that I thought had gone out of business. I discovered in reading that *Post* account of Perle's operations that one of his most controversial business connections, with publisher Conrad M. Black, came about through a meeting at precisely that evidently still vibrant elite venue.

Black headed up Hollinger International Inc., a vast conglomerate of mostly media companies. As the *Post* reported, "Perle joined Hollinger's board in 1994, having met Black at an annual Bilderberg Conference, where members of the international business and foreign policy elite meet to network and discuss issues." Perle's presence on the board of a company that published major newspapers including the *Chicago Sun-Times* and London's *Daily Telegraph*, along with many other electronic media outlets, put him in an even more important position to profit both personally and at the same time expand the reach of his foreign policy views. Perle also became a board member of the *Jerusalem Post*, another newspaper in the Hollinger group.

On the foreign policy side, I feel no confidence yet in assessing the degree to which Perle's views are driven by an interventionist ideology or by business associations from which he can profit. Some who have written about Perle suggest he is simply a pro-Israel hawk, and all else follows. I don't agree, because he often follows a course that is at odds with Israel's security interests by favoring policies that benefit states like Saudi Arabia, which have nurtured a religious fanaticism intrinsically hostile to Israel. Objectively, policies supported by Perle, certainly the second Gulf War, which empowered pro-Iranian Shiites quite opposed to Israel, were hardly a favor to the security of the Jewish state. What does seem to be a real connection here, however, is identification with the more hawkish hard-line Israeli camp, with Perle sharing its contempt for the torturous peace process, but that can be more logically explained as kindred souls in the worship of militarism than any primacy of importance attached to the well-being of Israel.

Those two sides to Perle were on display on one of the Hollinger-financed trips he made with Conrad Black on a company jet in the mid-1990s, when they visited both the crown prince of Jordan and Israeli Prime Minister Benjamin Netanyahu. Of course it is well documented that close ties exist among Perle, other neocons, and Netanyahu; indeed, some of the neocons worked in Netanyahu's electoral campaigns. But is the interest here in the Israeli leader any different than in the crown prince of Jordan, whom Perle was courting as a potential convert to a stronger pro-Western and pro-U.S. military stance than had been assumed by the prince's father, the often prickly and independent King Hussein?

On the profit side, Perle was made chairman and chief executive officer of Hollinger Digital, where he was paid $300,000 a year plus $3.1 million in bonuses according to the *Post* account and related lawsuits. That is startling compensation for Perle to have received while presiding over a subsidiary that managed to lose $65 million.

Perle also profited from his Hollinger connection after he joined with Gerald Paul Hillman, a New York investor, to found Trireme Partners L.P., the venture capital investment fund seeking to exploit the possibilities of investing in homeland securities technologies in the wake of the 9/11 tragedy. No jokes here about ambulance chasers, but it is interesting that at the very time Perle was hyping the threat of international terrorism, which he largely had ignored before 9/11, he was making a very good buck off of it. He managed to get Hollinger's Black to commit to a $25 million investment in Trireme, of which $2.5 million was paid. Neither Hollinger's board, on which Perle sat on the executive committee, nor the audit committee voted to approve that investment.

In 2004, a special outside audit committee, led by former SEC chairman Richard Breeden, examined Hollinger's losses and accused both Black and Perle of corruption. Black was forced out as CEO and Perle resigned from the board in 2006. The audit committee accused Perle of "flagrant abdication of duty" and of "putting his own interests above those of Hollinger's shareholders."

Auditors found $32 million in questionable payments to executives and investments Hollinger made in companies run by some of its board members, including the $2.5 million payment made by Hollinger Digital Inc., of which Perle was chairman and CEO, to Trireme Partners, of which Perle was managing partner.

In October 2006 the Securities and Exchange Commission notified Perle that he would not face civil charges for failing to notice fraud committed by the company's senior executives. Perle's lawyer told Bloomberg "There was absolutely no basis for [the allegations against Perle]."

A Salon.com article by Eric Boehlert published November 26, 2003, about the scandal quoted Nell Minow, editor of *The Corporate Library*, which covers corporate governance, to put the matter in perspective:

> It's typical of the problems many boards of directors face, but this seemed to be a case of board problems on steroids. The CEO had voting control, so there was not even pretense that shareholders had a role. He gets access to capital you only get

through going public, yet he gets to control it as
if it were a private company. For investors, it's the
worst of both worlds.

Whatever advice Perle gave Black, it did not help Black
avoid a criminal conviction and a prison sentence of six and a
half years for fraud and obstruction of justice. By then, Perle and
Black had become enemies, even though the association had left
Perle at least $5 million richer. Black earlier had accused Perle
of "nest-feathering . . . dissembling and obfuscation." Perle
continues to insist that Black misled him and that he had no
knowledge of any impropriety when he signed off on Black's
financial shenanigans.

Perle insists, as he always has in such matters, that there is no
conflict of interest between his pro-defense political stance and
his profiting from defense industry and other private companies
because he can maintain the proper ethical distance between the
two roles. Maybe he can, but a long history of dealing with such
matters has left the public and its representatives properly suspicious of such attempts at ethical self-policing. That is why there
is an ethics rule preventing individuals from using their government positions to advance their personal financial fortunes.

Did Perle violate that restriction when he recommended to
Defense Secretary Donald Rumsfeld that he place his Trireme
partner Hillman on the Defense Policy Board? Was it ethical for
Hillman, in a letter soliciting funds from the Boeing Company,
to mention that both he and his partner Perle were members of
that Pentagon board? Perle told the *Post* that it was necessary to
identify their Pentagon status because, "If we had not related
that information we would have been withholding information." Nice try, but it begs the question of whether Boeing was
more inclined to invest in a company because its two lead part-

ners were on a Pentagon board that had a great deal to do with advising on weapons programs in which Boeing had a stake.

But it should also be noted that Boeing was just doing the defense contractor thing, turning influence within the government into enormous profit in what is euphemistically called the "private sector." A report issued in 2004 by the Center for Public Integrity ("Outsourcing the Pentagon: Who Benefits from the Politics and Economics of National Security?") stated that Boeing was only the second largest recipient of Pentagon contracts, totaling nearly $82 billion in fiscal years 1998–2003. Number one, the Lockheed Martin Corporation, was awarded $94 billion in contracts in that same period.

Chapter 5

LIGHTING A CANDLE FOR WAR

No company was better positioned to take advantage of the moment of 9/11 than Lockheed Martin, the defense industry giant formed by the 1995 merger of the Lockheed Corporation and the Martin Marietta Corporation. Lockheed had thereby become the nation's top defense contractor and would, more than any other—including Dick Cheney's former company, Halliburton—profit from the fresh opportunity afforded by the new "war." Not that Halliburton was hurting. The Center for Public Integrity, in a November 19, 2007, report titled "Baghdad Bonanza," by Bill Buzenberg, noted that from 2004 to 2006, KBR, Inc., previously known as Kellogg, Brown, and Root and until April 5, 2007, was a Halliburton subsidiary, was awarded more than $16 billion in U.S. government contracts for work in Iraq and Afghanistan. Not to gainsay the significance of $16 billion, but it pales in comparison to loot garnered by the manufacturers of traditional big-ticket weapons systems. The ability of Lockheed Martin to help shape the president's response to 9/11 is typical of the feeding frenzy that followed in the tragedy's aftermath.

The challenge to defense contractors such as Lockheed Martin was to demonstrate that the high-tech equipment in which they specialized, which was designed to thwart a hostile state in possession of a sophisticated arsenal, was relevant to defeating a stateless band of terrorists. The three states that could be connected with al Qaeda did not easily fit the bill. The Taliban regime that controlled most of Afghanistan and had provided a base for Osama bin Laden had been all too easily defeated by the U.S. invasion. It was ludicrous to suggest that ratcheting up Cold War weaponry was useful in pursuing the remnants of either the Taliban or al Qaeda still operating in the tribal areas across the Pakistan-Afghanistan border. The three states that had diplomatically recognized the Taliban government in Afghanistan and provided support for the Taliban—Pakistan, United Arab Emirates, and Saudi Arabia—were all too quickly embraced by President Bush as allies rather than enemies, and quickly were removed as enemy targets for the new Cold War.

The answer to that need for a formidable enemy was found in the specter of a defanged Saddam Hussein, totally hemmed in by sanctions and U.S. dominance of the airways and shipping lanes critical to his country, who became resurrected as the new global menace. Thanks to an intense propaganda blitz, Saddam was recast as a modern-day Adolf Hitler in command of a fearsome military machine armed with weapons of mass destruction and in cahoots with al Qaeda. That this picture was known to administration hawks to be nonsense did not in any way inhibit the propagandists inside the Bush administration and their corporate allies eager for a new bogeyman to link it to the war on terror.

Among those corporate allies of the new fear campaign, none

was more enthusiastic than Bruce P. Jackson, a top executive at Lockheed Martin. The nation's leading defense contractor was in the process of wrapping up the biggest military contract in history for the F-35 joint fighter plane, with an eventual price tag of $300 billion. Jackson is another of those ambitious revolving door intellectuals who move easily from a military or other government position to the corporate world and back.

For a decade prior to 9/11, it was not easy to be a defense contractor, and it must have seemed to Bruce Jackson that he had gone through the wrong revolving door. Back in 1986, when he was an officer in military intelligence assigned to the Pentagon, Ronald Reagan was president and the Cold War was still very much in vogue. Military budgets were at an all-time high, and the acquisition fervor in the Pentagon to buy ever more complex and expensive weapons had at least a somewhat plausible purpose. Then the Cold War ended all too abruptly, and the new president, George Herbert Walker Bush, was cutting back what had suddenly come to be widely criticized as the Pentagon's overblown budget. The military-industrial complex was cast into the deepest gloom, and Jackson tried to pursue a civilian course. Mustering out of Pentagon service, he went to work briefly for a Wall Street investment house, but that didn't last long.

Military defense is Jackson's game, and he soon landed a job in more familiar terrain with defense contractor Martin Marietta, where he became director for strategic planning. He had a high-paying job and a fine title, but he quickly discovered that his new employer was in big trouble. The end of the Cold War had been disastrous for the previously high-riding defense companies, and corporate cutbacks and consolidation were suddenly the norm. Because of the cutbacks, his company merged with Lockheed.

Jackson did well at the new company, where he started as director of defense planning and analysis, but complex and expensive new weapons systems were a tough sell after the end of the Cold War. Jackson decided to do something about it. Americans needed to be jolted out of their false sense of security. The public had been deluded by the Soviet Union's collapse into thinking there were no big defense needs out there just because there was no comparable enemy in sight. Instead of cursing the darkness of peacetime, Bruce Jackson lit a candle for war.

Sure, he could have accepted the paradigm switch to another occupation to better beat swords into plowshares as America began to enjoy the peace dividend made possible by the end of a half century of real and impending catastrophic global war. Instead, he dug in his heels and did extensive pro-military-spending outreach in the public arena, including writing the key foreign policy plank for the Republican Party in 2000, when he served as chair of the platform subcommittee on foreign policy, all while still very much on the Lockheed payroll.

There is nothing particularly conspiratorial about the role Bruce Jackson played in attempting to stoke the passion for defense spending in the bleak season before 9/11 or going wild in capitalizing upon the enormous opportunity presented by that tragedy for defense contractors. Exploiting our fears is what defense contractors do for a living. Jackson is significant not because of his pushing public policies that benefited the corporation he worked for but rather because he proved so effective in manufacturing the consent for war that both of his previous employers so desperately sought. That he lined his own pockets in the process may be less important in his mind's eye than that he simultaneously served a militaristic ideological crusade that he had come to fervently endorse.

Jackson is typical of that small band of defense intellectuals who have profited from their patriotic fervor while exploiting the fears of a nation as to the clear and present danger posed by its foreign enemies, imaginary or real. When he first entered the game as an eager young army intelligence officer back in the early Reagan years, Jackson managed to catch the approving eyes of seasoned hawks at the Pentagon, particularly his bosses, Richard Perle, Paul Wolfowitz, and Dick Cheney. They all had been appointed by Reagan and were eager to inflame the confrontations of the Cold War that they believed had been tamed in the era of détente under President Richard Nixon.

When that ride ended and Jackson found himself working for defense contractors, he turned to his old Pentagon bosses for inspiration and found it in the Project for the New American Century, which he helped them launch. Now reborn as neoconservatives, Jackson and the other Pentagon hawks would work mightily with others of their ilk to turn the nation away from the expectation of a peace dividend and to a new resolve to spend even more money on the preparation for a future war. A century of such preparation is what they had in mind, as they quite candidly proclaimed in the title for their new organization: the Project for the New American Century.

The task that they set out to accomplish was daunting: to claim credit for the dissolution of the Soviet enemy as a consequence of the huge military buildup of the Reagan years, which they had helped create, while justifying increased defense spending, despite the sudden absence of that enemy. The story of how they came to seize upon the trauma of the 9/11 attacks to launch a new "global war on terror" now has been well told. But back then in the 1990s, in making the case for keeping the nation on permanent war footing, the enemy as terrorist was barely mentioned. Instead, they stirred the pot of familiar Cold War–era alarms—the twin menaces of Red China and North

Korea, and the purported allies of those still surviving and therefore useful communist regimes among the freelance dictators found in Libya, Iran, Syria, and, of course, Iraq.

In the initial proclamation of PNAC, there is scant mention of the stateless terrorists like Osama bin Laden, who already had killed Americans in bold acts of terrorism and a few years later pulled off the 9/11 attacks. But from the point of reference of Bruce Jackson, sitting at his desk at Lockheed Martin, that omission makes perfect sense. The uncomfortable truth concerning the arms manufacturers and their partners in the Defense Department is that what they do, and what they sell, really has very little, if anything, to do with countering the terrorist enemy. No knowledgeable person could honestly make the case that more F-22 fighters or B-2 bombers would be effective in rooting out stateless terrorists.

Later, they would try to make those weapons seem vitally significant with the wildly irrelevant, indeed counterproductive, bombing runs over Afghanistan which, as should have been expected, proved useless in fulfilling the president's stated pledge of capturing bin Laden dead or alive. But the good news for Jackson was that as ineffective and yet expensive as that exercise was, the public didn't notice. Nor did the irrelevance of the "shock and awe" campaign to depose Saddam Hussein less than a year and a half later—which allowed defense contractors to trot out even more of their advanced weaponry—detract from the enormous "we are back in business" relief felt at the headquarters of Lockheed Martin and other centers of the military-industrial complex.

Lockheed had every right to expect close ties to the incoming Bush administration. Thomas Donnelly, former deputy executive director of PNAC and the main author of the PNAC report that justified increased defense spending, was hired to work for the company. He was not alone; in the run-up to the Iraq war, no fewer than eight key players with ties to Lockheed were connected with the Bush administration. Lynne Cheney, the vice president's wife, served as a member of Lockheed's board of directors from 1994 until January 2001, and as *The Multinational Monitor* reported in its January/February 2003 issue, she accumulated "more than $500,000 in deferred director's fees in the process. Former Lockheed [President and] Chief Operating Officer Peter Teets is now Undersecretary of the Air Force and Director of the National Reconnaissance Office, a post that includes making decisions on the acquisition of everything from reconnaissance satellites to space-based elements of missile defense."

Not surprisingly, Lockheed, along with the other major arms makers, was an immediate beneficiary of the post-9/11 increase of the military budget for weapons that had no direct connection to the 9/11 attacks. During its first two years in office, before the Iraq invasion, the Bush administration already had requested $150 billion in new defense spending, and while Congress had granted most of that, questions were starting to arise about what in the world the F-22 Raptor and the other advanced systems that Lockheed and its fellow merchants were being paid for had to do with fighting terrorists. The invasion of Afghanistan had been hailed as a great success for the modern U.S. military machine, but the rabble of terrorists had escaped largely intact and, indeed, soon gave proof of renewed strength. There was only so much bombing of Afghan mountains that the media was willing to thrill to and Congress to finance.

No one really believed either that Afghanistan would be pacified after centuries of failure by other foreigners to accomplish that task—or that it mattered. To understand the shift in attention from the crucial terrorist spawning ground overlapping the Pakistan-Afghanistan border, which had everything to do with 9/11, to Iraq, which didn't, one must reference not the national security threat but rather the threat to the power, prestige, and profit of the military-industrial complex. Afghanistan failed as a target of opportunity, whereas Iraq would perform splendidly.

Al Qaeda–style terrorists do not do "theater wars," preferring, as we learned on 9/11, to pop up unannounced in the enemy's backyard. That was the problem in treating Afghanistan as a theater of war; the Taliban remained because they were an indigenous force preoccupied with restoring their power in their own country. The terrorists they had harbored simply vanished, to reappear without regard to a clearly demarcated theater of operation. That harsh reality presented a huge problem for those eager to have far-flung theaters of battle to justify a new military buildup, and it explains the real need to have gone to war with Iraq.

The invasion of Iraq was key because, as the Soviets had learned, massive military power in Afghanistan never would be effective in subduing the fanatics among the Afghan populace or providing a raison d'être for one's modern military apparatus. As Rumsfeld ruefully complained, "there are no good targets" in Afghanistan. Nor is there any resource, other than the verboten opium crop, that might in any conceivable sense ever pay for this never-ending fireworks display. Iraq was the necessary battlefield—a quick victory could be ensured, more so certainly than with an attack on Iran, and the oil revenue would pay for the cost of war and occupation.

Quite naturally, even five years before 9/11, Iraq was mentioned most prominently as the target of opportunity for exploiting America's fears. Not surprisingly, in late 2002, Bruce Jackson sprang into action as head of yet another propaganda outfit, this time serving as chairman of the Committee for the Liberation of Iraq. Jackson told *American Prospect* editor John B. Judis in a January 1, 2003, interview "People in the White House said, 'We need you to do for Iraq what you did for NATO.'"

That request is quite telling; what Jackson had done for NATO was to help provide an organization that, with the demise of the Soviet enemy, no longer had any reason for existence with a new sense of purpose and a much-expanded roster of member nations drawn from the old Soviet satellite states. It was no small feat to convince the other NATO powers, particularly France and Germany, that they needed the likes of Latvia and Estonia as partners to help them guard against the former Soviet Union.

There was one lure: The requirement for joining NATO is that new members' military forces have to be reequipped with modern weapons systems, most of which is supplied by the United States and our allies. The single largest beneficiary of this force modernization was Lockheed Martin, where Jackson was hanging his hat. The new NATO nations particularly object to the cost of their weapons upgrades, since U.S. taxpayers paid for most of it.

Such wheeling and dealing on the part of defense contractors is all too common, but some did notice the benefits to Lockheed from Jackson's NATO organizing. As Jeff Gerth and Tim Weiner reported in the *New York Times*, June 29, 1997: "At night Bruce L. Jackson is president of the U.S. Committee to Expand NATO, giving intimate dinners for senators and foreign officials. By day, he is director of strategic planning for Lockheed Martin Corporation, the world's biggest weapons maker." But references to such apparent conflicts of interest are a media rarity, and they certainly did not deter Jackson, who was a Bush delegate to the 2000 Republican National Convention and a key author of the party's platform on foreign policy, as he had been four years before. Clearly what was good for Lockheed was presumed to be good for the GOP and, by extension, America as a whole.

A win-win deal all around, except for U.S. taxpayers, and even they could be pacified with the evidence in 2003 that NATO membership also guaranteed uncritical support for U.S. policy toward Iraq from those Eastern European member countries. The list of the "coalition of the willing" nations is a tribute to Jackson's being able to get some payback for his NATO shenanigans.

Jackson had no compunction about working the NATO expansion deal that benefited Lockheed while on the company's payroll, nor did the U.S. media devote much space to this apparent, actually obvious, conflict of interest, NATO expansion not being one of those sexy subjects that garners media attention. But it didn't hurt Jackson's career at Lockheed, where he was named vice president for strategy and planning in 1999, thanks in part to his work on NATO expansion.

It wasn't until Jackson left Lockheed in 2002 to form the new pro-war Iraq committee that his name and past activities surfaced. This was partially due to the awkwardness of complaints in the media of those former Soviet satellite countries that the uncritical support of their leaders for Bush's war policy represented a payback for NATO admission that might not fully serve their nations' security interests. That point was made more evident by the deaths of Eastern European troops in Iraq, a country that had certainly never threatened the security of Poland or other Eastern European nations.

As Judis pointed out in *American Prospect's* April 30, 2003, issue, Jackson, like his mentor Richard Perle, was perceived as having an official role in the new Bush administration quite apart from any title. Jackson's lobbying was not hindered by a specific Pentagon title, but he was bestowed with an unofficial one by Bush administration officials. As Judis reported:

> With Bush's election, foreign governments began to treat Jackson as a representative of the administration. "I would call him the unofficial U.S. ambassador to NATO," said Vigodas Usackas, the Lithuanian ambassador to the United States. Georgia's President Eduard Shevardnadze described Jackson after a visit as "an official with clout, someone whose opinion is heeded in Europe and in the United States." U.S. Ambassador to NATO Nicholas Burns called him "an indispensable part of our efforts in reaching out to these [former Soviet bloc] governments."

Jackson parlayed his leverage with the administration in enlisting the support of the Eastern European countries for Bush's Iraq policy. "They clearly wanted to do stuff to impress upon the U.S. Senate [which had to approve NATO membership], the freedom-fighting credentials of these new democracies," Jackson told the *International Herald Tribune*. However, for some in those countries, Jackson's heavy-handed lobbying hardly seemed like an extension of their own freedom, as in Slovenia, where the prime minster later said it was a mistake to have signed on to the pro-U.S. statement. One prominent journalist commented that the government there had "buckled under . . . Bruce Jackson's threat."

Jackson had no regrets, viewing the support he enlisted from Eastern Europe as a necessary counter to the objections raised by long-standing U.S. allies over the admission to NATO of the former communist bloc countries: "The idea was to break the Franco-German monopoly over shaping European foreign policy," Jackson told the *Financial Times*. "If France and Germany can tell other Europeans what to do, we can do the same."

The problem, as Judis pointed out in that 2003 article, was that the easy equation of Jackson's agenda with that of the United States indicated by the royal "we" should be a matter of concern:

> Whatever one thinks of NATO expansion and the war in Iraq, it should be clear that something is very wrong here. NATO expansion is not necessarily a bad thing. And some countries may have wanted to endorse the American invasion of Iraq. But the Bush administration shouldn't be holding entry into NATO hostage to support for its war in Iraq, or trying to gull the public about the size of its "coalition of the willing." Even worse, it shouldn't be getting a private citizen—with no accountability to the public, the Congress or even the administration itself—to do its dirty work. Will it take the Bush administration's equivalent of the Iran-Contra scandal to stop these kinds of practices?

The answer is no, because under George W. Bush whatever had remained of the line between the interests of profit-seeking corporations and individuals and U.S. national security requirements had been totally obliterated, a process that was more often abetted than challenged by the Democratic opposition.

Chapter 6

PLEASE PASS THE PORK

Who doesn't like pork? When it comes to tagging the federal budget with those infamous "earmarks" that target taxpayer dollars for special, and most often dubious, expenditures back in one's home district, the list is bipartisan and ranges broadly from liberal to conservative. Earmarks for military spending that supports jobs and profits back home, not to mention campaign contributions, are particularly attractive because a member of Congress can cloak narrow ambition in the guise of patriotic fervor. As the general-turned-president Dwight Eisenhower warned in his seminal 1961 military-industrial complex speech, the "defense establishment" is spread throughout the country, and so too are the politicians who therefore support it.

Take the case of one of the Senate's most liberal—even antiwar—Democratic members, California's Barbara Boxer, and the $1.6 billion tucked into the 2007 budget for Boeing's C-17 Globemaster III, a pricey transport plane the Pentagon had not asked for. Indeed, the Pentagon had requested $300 million, not to build even more such aircraft but rather to cover the cost of mothballing the C-17 production line and ending production once the last of the original allotment of 180 planes rolled off the assembly line in Long Beach, California, in 2009. But some Air Force procurement folks did an end-run around their higher-ups and leaked a wish list to friends of the C-17 in Congress, asking for that $1.6 billion to build seven more.

This was such a blatant circumvention of the Pentagon hierarchy that three prominent senators, Republican John McCain of Arizona, Democrat Edward M. Kennedy of Massachusetts, and Democrat Thomas R. Carper of Delaware, were motivated to express their outrage in a letter to the Air Force complaining about this subversion of the normal budgeting process. On September 11, 2007, McCain complained in writing that he was "troubled by the Air Force's apparent disregard for proper acquisition policy, practice and procedure and seeming eagerness to further contractors' interests."

His colleague Boxer did not seem a bit troubled; on the contrary, her spokesman, David Sandretti, told the *Los Angeles Daily News* that the senator wouldn't stop at seven more of the unneeded aircraft and would demand a total of forty-two more, at $250 million a pop. Using the leaked wish list as his prop, Sandretti stated: "This is a significant development because the Air Force has stated in no uncertain terms that this is one of their top priorities. Unfortunately, the budget writers in the administration didn't get that message."

Neither did Dick Cheney back in April 1990, when the then secretary of defense made the decision to cut the intended production of 210 C-17s down to 120. Cheney's sensible decision was made as part of a general review by the first Bush administration of weapons needs in light of the end of the Cold War. The pre-Halliburton Cheney was more like his previous boss,

Bush I, a traditional fiscal conservative, than the profligate Bush II, who after 9/11 opened the floodgates on military spending.

Cheney was right the first time. There just wasn't any real need for the plane in military terms. The existing C-5 transport aircraft could carry twice as many troops as the new C-17, and even rebuilding them would cost far less than the $250 million each in the 2008 budget. The lobby for the C-17, representing Boeing and the local unions and politicians in the Long Beach area, kept trying despite Cheney's rejection, and under Bill Clinton there were renewed efforts to expand the program beyond the forty already ordered. But in 1995, the General Accounting Office (GAO), which is charged in our system of governance with providing nonpartisan objective advice that legislators hungry for pork tend to ignore, suggested a further cut.

The GAO was asked by Congress to evaluate the request of the Pentagon, then under the Clinton administration, for 120 C-17s and found that it was three times too many: "A fleet of forty C-17s and 64 commercial freighters could meet the Defense Department's airlift requirements . . . at a cost savings of upwards of $10 billion when compared to a fleet of 120 C-17s," according to the January 26, 1995, GAO report.

As happens with every effort to cut a weapons program, it seems we can't just give that money to Boeing's workers who might lose their jobs if the C-17 line is shut down in Long Beach, California, although even a small fraction of the tens of billions spent on the C-17 would go a long way toward easing the pain of the 11,000 Long Beach workers while their company developed another, more needed type of aircraft. But defense money in hand is a lot better than pie-in-the-sky promises of job training or other efforts to aid those workers, and the unions that represent them joined with the company to pressure politicians to keep the C-17 planes rolling.

Boxer had gone to the Long Beach plant as part of the "Red Team" lobbying coalition that included union and Boeing managers, Long Beach City Council members, the mayor, local business leaders, California's governor, its other U.S. senator, and various members of the House. The House members supporting the plane ranged across the political spectrum, including far right Republican Congressman Dana Rohrabacher of Orange County, who tends to support federal spending only when it involves the military; ditto for GOP Congressman Duncan Hunter of San Diego, who was a very influential chairman of the House Armed Services Committee, and Jerry Lewis, another hawkish Republican congressman representing San Bernardino County. Boxer was not the only Democrat who joined the cause. Senator Dianne Feinstein and at least four local Democratic members of Congress were on the C-17 cheerleading squad.

The pitch to save the plane was all about jobs, jobs, jobs, and rarely was there reference to a national defense need for the transport or to the less savory matter of Boeing's profits. As a case in point, take California Governor Arnold Schwarzenegger's rallying visit to the Long Beach plant on September 26, 2006. At the event, the governor never mentioned any need for the planes other than as a source of jobs. He began by bragging of his success in increasing the number of jobs in California, before a storm cloud appeared:

> But a year ago I got the bad news. I got a phone call from Jim Albaugh, your CEO of Boeing, and of David Bowman [the C-17 program manager for Boeing]. They both called me and they said, "I think there is a danger here that the federal government may not continue with our contract, that

we maybe have to shut down our plant, that we discontinue building our C-17s, that 11,000 people may lose their jobs."

So we started a campaign, all the Congressional leaders, our Congressional delegation from California, our office, everyone started working and started that campaign, sending letters to the federal government, making phone calls, and doing everything that we could do to reverse their decision, to make sure to keep that plant open, to make sure to continue building the C-17, to make sure that we continue the 11,000 jobs right here in Long Beach [6,500 exclusively on the C-17].

It was a line perfectly accompanied by applause.

Imagine Schwarzenegger and the other politicians, Democrats and Republicans, using all of that collective political clout to save jobs that were not national security–related. It seems downright socialistic and even somewhat out of character for Schwarzenegger, who almost torpedoed his career by angering nurses, firefighters, teachers, and law enforcement with his stingy approach to their budget requests. But federal money for defense workers was another matter, and that day at the Long Beach plant, his words seemed so heartfelt and concerned with the well-being of the workers that it was startling to suddenly hear a Republican governor showing such enormous sympathy for the plight of the potentially unemployed:

And I'm very happy to say today that we're going to continue building the C-17 and continue keeping the eleven thousand jobs so you can continue working, because that is extremely

important, that you all have a job. Because when
it comes to jobs, it's not just that you lose money
when you lose a job. But people, when they are
jobless, when they are on unemployment, they
don't feel good. They don't feel productive. They
don't feel wanted. . . . And this is why I'm going to
fight all the way to the end to make sure that you
keep your jobs right here in Long Beach and keep
building the C-17.

What this really is all about is welfare for defense companies
and a government-sponsored jobs program for their workers
under the guise of building planes at $250 million each that the
Pentagon has not requested. But it was a good time for Schwarzenegger to be at the C-17 plant because, once again, the plane
had received a reprieve. And although the Pentagon had tried to
kill the program with its budget submission in the early spring,
here in the fall of 2006, the House-Senate conference committee with both Republican and Democratic votes had added $2.1
billion, more than Boxer initially requested, for an additional
ten C-17s.

But the main reason that money continued to be doled out
for the C-17 had far less to do with the job security of Boeing's
workers and far more to do with Boeing's corporate profits.
Obviously, Boeing has the ability to make splendid civilian
commercial aircraft, and one would have hoped that they,
being far better at commercial work than the other leading
defense contractors, would have led the way in refocusing the
defense industry after the end of the Cold War to reap the long-
promised peace dividend. But even Boeing had become hooked
on the easier buck to be made from the military.

An article in the April 30, 1999, *Seattle Post-Intelligencer* pointed out that ". . . the C-17 has become Boeing's most profitable large airplane." The profit margin on C-17 sales ran around 13 percent, while Boeing's commercial production on the 747, the company's most profitable commercial plane, was producing a profit margin of less than 5 percent. The pressure on the commercial side vastly increased two years later, after the 9/11 attacks, when civilian passenger traffic fell sharply.

On the other hand, 9/11 and the ensuing wars in Afghanistan and Iraq provided a grand opportunity for ramping up the sales of military aircraft as the defense budget more than doubled within the next three years. But although Boeing's other military planes, particularly the F-22, a joint project with Lockheed, did very well, the C-17 was left hanging. The fact that the Pentagon didn't want to fund this plane when it was throwing money at just about every other defense industry offering was a measure of how little need there was for it.

In recent years, new funding for the plane was not just left out of the budget as a bit of Pentagon forgetfulness. Rather, it was omitted as a result of the calculated findings of the Defense Department's quadrennial review in 2006, a projection of U.S. military needs over the next twenty years. The DOD review concluded that the 180th C-17, due to be finally assembled after the contract's expiration and already funded in previous budgets, would serve the national security just fine.

But Boxer, who normally favors defense spending cuts, abruptly changed course when it came to jobs in her own state. In the case of the C-17, she roundly condemned the Pentagon for not wanting to spend more. "I don't know what they're thinking. This makes no sense whatsoever," Boxer groused without challenging the Pentagon's assessment in any substantive way other than insisting that top Air Force officials believed, as the *Long Beach Press-Telegram* put it in a story February 23, 2006, headlined, "Sen. Boxer in the Ring for Boeing C-17," ". . . the post-Sept. 11 terror attacks would require a minimum of forty-two new C-17s to go with the 180 now under contract and being built."

Not content with the more than $45 billion already spent on the plane, Boxer wanted to throw another $10 billion down that sinkhole. This from a senator who would end up losing to the administration, a year later, on extending child health insurance to four million uninsured kids because Bush claimed the $7 billion annual cost was too great.

Surely Boxer knew that the massive military expenditure piling up would deprive funds for such needed social programs in the future. Yet the liberal senator never made the argument that some of the excess in Pentagon spending, particularly for a program like the C-17 that even Bush couldn't justify, could be used to pay for children's health care.

Boxer's reasoning is odd: The main value of the C-17 in the post-9/11 world had been its use in ferrying a huge amount of equipment to Iraq to fight a war that Boxer opposed as having nothing to do with combating 9/11-style terrorist attacks. But even if one accepted the necessity of fighting wars like the one in Iraq, which the Pentagon planners certainly did, it was also true that much of the material flown into Iraq to support the oc-cupation came via commercial aircraft. Since U.S. control of the skies over Iraq was total, it was also possible for standard FedEx and United Parcel Service deliveries to be made.

However, the best means of supplying an occupation in a foreign land, if that is our goal, would be through transoceanic shipping, which is how 90 percent of supplies did enter Iraq. Former *Washington Post* reporter Vernon Loeb made this clear in an October 24, 2003, *Post* article after flying into Baghdad airport aboard one of the C-17s that cost $5,458 an hour to fly.

This particular plane brought in shock absorbers, tires, and engine oil at a cost far greater than delivering those same products by ship, although shipping did take longer:

> While C-17s from Charleston and C-5 Galaxies from Dover Air Force Base, Del., fly hundreds of tons of cargo a day to the Iraqi theater, airlift is responsible for only 10 percent of the materiel needed to support the military effort. Ninety percent goes by ship, which is fast enough for nonpriority loads—and far cheaper. The time difference is eighteen hours by air vs. nineteen days by ship. The price difference to send a single meal ready to eat, or MRE: $7 by air, 7 cents by sea. Since Sept. 11, 2001, military aircraft and civilian contractors such as FedEx and UPS have hauled almost 1 million passengers and 240,000 tons of materiel to the Iraq and Afghan theaters. "It's like moving the entire city of Indianapolis—all the people, all their cars, all their buses, everything they own and everything it takes to sustain them."

That one paragraph cuts through all of the posturing by Boxer and her congressional allies in earmarking funding for more of the C-17s that had already cost taxpayers over $45 billion. Send it by FedEx, by ship, or one of the hundreds of military cargo planes we already have—the military does not need any more C-17s, period. In the House, the six Republicans and one Democrat who sponsored the C-17 earmark had received more than $72,000 from Boeing and its employees in campaign contributions during the previous two years. But in Senator Boxer's case, the motivation for her support of the plane was said by those close to her—and by Boxer herself—to stem not from the minimal financial support she receives from the defense industry but far more from her concern for the well-being of the workers in the Boeing plant whose jobs were at stake.

It is precisely this ability of the defense industry to play off the interests of its workers and the communities in which they shop and live to irrationally influence spending that creates the kind of waste that Eisenhower warned about. Both the plane's supporters, as well as some of its detractors, seem to be motivated less by national security concerns than by what's good for jobs and profit in their districts. The *St. Louis Post-Dispatch* noted these competing allegiances on October 31, 2007, as a last-minute attempt was made to stash money for the plane in yet another earmark to save it:

> The plane has friends in Congress, where dozens of lawmakers have C-17 work in their districts and where ten House members . . . stuck $2.4 billion for ten more into a budget earmark. But it also has skeptics in high places . . . who represent districts where the Air Force's other large cargo plane, the C-5, is based, and who would rather see those aging planes refurbished than spend money on new C-17s.

The use of the word "aging" might have been unintentional in stacking the argument in favor of the C-17, which happens to be built, in part, in the area serviced by the newspaper. It is true that the C-5 is older, but the counterargument is that it could be totally refurbished at a much lower cost than building a new plane, and that the "aging" C-5 could carry a much larger cargo than the newer C-17.

In frustration that the debate was about everything but national security, the Armed Services Committee's Democratic chairman, Congressman Ike Skelton of Missouri, criticized the Air Force secretary, who testified to his committee in an ambiguous way, destined apparently to pacify both sides. Chairman Ike complained, "I've heard no word about strategic thought or where the Air Force should be in the strategic position for our country."

Once again, the Air Force tried to have it both ways, pretending to go along with the secretary of defense's request while leaking its wish list to sympathetic members of Congress to push specific planes, including the C-17, that serve the economic interests of their contributors and constituents.

As one senior Air Force official told the *Washington Post* in an October 16, 2007, article: "The Air Force doesn't have the money for the C-17s . . . if someone wants to give it to us, we'll certainly take it."

As it turned out, the end run the Air Force attempted in Congress was thwarted, and there was no money allocated in the 2008 budget for the C-17. But a new gimmick called the supplementary budget for the Iraq and Afghanistan wars had come into play. Even though, as we have seen, the C-17 was hardly essential to fighting those wars, it still was possible to provide funding for that plane and other favored projects in the almost $200 billion supplementary funding. That amount was beyond the $480 billion of the regular defense budget in fiscal year 2008. And supporting the troops meant that items in the supplementary budget would receive less scrutiny than those in the regular Defense Department allocation.

Representative John Murtha (D-PA), chairman of the House Appropriations Subcommittee on Defense and one of the all-time masters of the military funding earmark, promised supporters of the plane that help was on the way. As *Defense Daily*, a trade journal, put it in a November 8, 2007, story, referring to the exclusion of the C-17 and another plane, the C-130J, which had not made the cut in the final Congressional Conference Committee report: "The report does not address funding for additional C-17 Globemaster aircraft by Boeing or C-130J by Lockheed Martin. But Murtha said the House is likely to recommend adding ten C-17s and a number of C-130Js to the supplemental that lawmakers will consider next year."

"Next year" meant in 2008, when all members of the House and many senators were up for reelection, and it would be a safe bet that members of Congress who wanted those planes to increase their election chances would have their way.

The exercise of funding a plane that the Pentagon had not requested involved cynicism on all sides, including Congress, industry lobbyists, and the Pentagon itself. As Winslow Wheeler, a longtime insider in this game who is now one of the sharpest critics of Pentagon waste at the Center for Defense Information, put it on February 14, 2006, in a briefing critiquing the game played by Rumsfeld on his last budget request:

> Secretary of Defense Rumsfeld has requested a budget he knows Congress will augment and expand. Proposals to reduce the Army Reserve and National Guard, to truncate C-17 production, and to retire prematurely the F-117 "stealth" bomber (and other proposals), are what some call "Washington Monument Drills" ("WMDs," they are proposed budget reductions the Pentagon knows Congress will immediately add back into the budget). The thought that any such money will be saved is surely illusory.

In sum, in a time of war and when certain critical elements of the defense budget require steadfast
support and straightforward justification, today's
Pentagon leadership gives the nation mismatches
between rhetoric and realities and a focus on budget gimmicks.

The Pentagon can get away with this tactic because it can
rely on strong bipartisan support in Congress for supporting
weapons systems that the Pentagon fails to request. It counts
on the lobbyists who bankroll politicians and the constituents
whose jobs and profits are dependent on a particular weapon to
allocate the money even when the Pentagon did not ask for it.

For example, take Joe Lieberman, the Democratic Party's
vice presidential candidate in the 2000 election, whose Web
site bragged: "Lieberman Lauds Senate Approval of Nation's
Defense Blueprint. Leadership position benefits Connecticut's
defense workers."

Lieberman has been an ardent supporter of the Iraq war,
and while he is in part acting out of his own hawkish orientation, he makes it clear to his constituents that the war is also
a wonderful local jobs-and-profit program. Boasting after the
Senate approved the 2007 defense budget, Lieberman said, in a
September 30, 2006, press release, "The bill authorized funding of $462.8 billion in budget authority for defense programs
in fiscal year 2007, an increase of $21.2 billion—or 3.6% in real
terms—above the amount authorized by the Congress for fiscal
year 2006."

Noting that an additional $70 billion had been authorized
in emergency supplemental funding "in support of operations
in Iraq, Afghanistan, and the global war on terrorism," Lieberman's press release credited the senator for leading that effort:

"As a member of the Armed Services Committee and a ranking member of a key subcommittee, Lieberman played a crucial role in shaping the measure to make our soldiers safer and also strengthen Connecticut's defense industry and economy."

The press release then quoted Lieberman as saying,

> It is crucial that we invest the necessary resources for technology, training, weapons, and personnel that are essential to fighting the continued global war on terror. Connecticut defense companies are national leaders in providing our military with the sophisticated equipment and innovations needed to preserve our national security.

Pratt & Whitney is one of those Connecticut defense companies, and Lieberman went on to claim that the bill he helped push "added $1.4 billion for twenty F-22A Raptor fighter aircraft, which are powered by F119 Pratt and Whitney engines." The bill, he boasted, also authorized an additional multiyear contract for up to sixty F-22 aircraft over the next three years.

As for the C-17, even though the plane was built in Long Beach, there was still a Connecticut angle for Lieberman to support; he cited the "$4.4 billion to procure twenty-two C-17 strategic lift aircraft, which are powered by F117-PW-100 engines from Pratt & Whitney."

Who cares? After all, jobs were saved—so what that some defense companies got to report record profits? What harm is there in having more transport planes? The harm can only be assessed by judging the opportunity costs of those planes or determining what the money could have bought if spent on other programs. For some in Congress, there are no other programs beyond the needs of the military, and for them this question is irrelevant.

That sort of reasoning does not apply to Barbara Boxer, who, while supporting the C-17, often bemoans cuts in a number of domestic programs she considers vital. Indeed, when Bush's overall budget for 2008 was first announced at the beginning of 2007, Boxer denounced it in a press release under a heading on her Web site stating "Boxer: Bush Budget Ignores Priorities of the American People, Obscures True Costs of War in Iraq." She goes on to bemoan the woeful underfunding of all programs that help kids not born to well-off families: Head Start, after-school programs, and even President Bush's signature No Child Left Behind program. She goes on with a long list of such programs that are underfunded, from food safety to the Urban Indian Health Program.

Then, tucked inexplicably in the midst of complaints about lack of money for Medicare and firefighters, is this oddly placed item about the C-17s: "The President's budget includes no funds for the additional procurement of C-17 aircraft, which has been critical in airlifting troops and equipment during operations in Iraq and Afghanistan," the press release stated, followed by a quote from Boxer: "Continuing the production of these aircraft would not only ensure America has the best airlifter in the world, but also ensure that the jobs of the thousands of Californians who work on C-17s are not lost. I will be working with my colleagues to see that the C-17 line is not shuttered."

There you have it. A liberal senator who treats expenditures of billions of dollars on building more planes than the Pentagon can find a use for ends up defending it as a jobs program. She seems incapable, as are most Democrats in Congress, of grasping that the enormously swollen military budget may be draining resources from needed domestic programs. Or, to be less charitable, she probably understands it all too well, but political opportunism prevents her from challenging the wishes of the unions involved.

As for her tepid argument that the plane is "the best airlifter" (language from a Boeing press release) and is needed in the Iraq war (which she wanted to shut down), it is simply not worthy of consideration. Not when, as discussed above, the evidence is so overwhelming from the Iraq experience that the existing force, supplemented by private air delivery systems like FedEx and UPS, are more than up for the job and that, as was pointed out, 90 percent of the goods sent to Iraq came at a much lower cost by avoiding airlifting and using old-fashioned cargo ships.

All this is further proof that when it comes to the defense budget, there is strong bipartisan support for endless waste.

Chapter 7

$75 BILLION UNDER THE SEA

The one weapon that you don't need in the fight against terrorists is a new submarine with a $2.5 billion price tag that was designed to defeat Soviet subs in a battle to control the deep seas. The Soviets are gone, and what remains of their sub fleet in Russian hands is poorly maintained and rarely allowed to submerge for long journeys. So clearly, the fifty-two attack submarines kept by the United States at peak performance are without a worthy adversary, and one is not about to be launched by stateless terrorists like al Qaeda. You can't use a submarine to capture bin Laden in his cave or to prevent a potential skyjacker from crossing our borders to take flight training. This is why even the Bush Pentagon, ever eager to throw billions at almost any weapons system, no matter how archaic, drew the line at building more subs.

Yet there was Democratic Connecticut Senator Joseph Lieberman, almost five years after 9/11, insisting at a hearing of the Senate Armed Services Committee that despite all evidence to the contrary, "The submarine is not a Cold War legacy," and sounding the antiterrorist alarm that "[a] diminished submarine fleet cannot meet the demands of a post-9/11 world."

Now it happens that the submarines, including the latest edition, the Virginia class, are built by the Electric Boat Company, a division of General Dynamics, in Lieberman's home state, and that when he made those remarks on April 6, 2006, he was facing reelection. The loss of defense jobs was not good news for politicians courting Connecticut voters. As Lieberman testified: "The news only gets worse. It is anticipated that Electric Boat will be forced to lay off up to 2,400 additional workers before the end of the year."

But outside of the representatives from Virginia, the other state that produces submarines, Lieberman was aware that most other members of Congress would not endorse building more modern submarines as a jobs program, nor would they buy the argument that subs were needed to take out suicide bombers that might strike the New York subway system. Lieberman's argument that the Virginia-class submarine is "an indispensable weapon in our arsenal to fight the 'long war' on terrorism" was hardly convincing. So, after the obligatory reference to the "asymmetric challenges" represented by stateless terrorists and rogue nations, Lieberman was forced to invoke a more traditional enemy: the yellow horde of communist-run China.

The derogatory adjectives are left out these days, however, in deference to the fact that those same Chicoms, as we called the "Red" Chinese during the Cold War, now are carrying a large part of the U.S. debt incurred in building weapons we don't need. The joke is on us; we use the China scare to buy weapons to contain the menace of China, and those same Chinese profit from the interest they charge us on loans to pay for the weapons to contain them. It's win-win for the Chinese communists, U.S. politicians, defense contractors, and their workforce—in short, everyone except the typical U.S. taxpayer, who pays but doesn't get to win in this game.

Lieberman's defense of his bid for the submarines to be built in Connecticut, once he dispensed with the convenient exhortations concerning the terrorist threat, was to point out that the Chinese can build products other than the ones you find on the shelves of Wal-Mart and Costco. Not that anyone would want to buy a vastly inferior sub from the Chinese on the world market, but that didn't stop Lieberman from sounding the "Chinese are coming" alarm that has worked so effectively throughout American history in panicking voters: "The Chinese are designing new classes of submarines with increased capabilities," Lieberman thundered, adding darkly, "If we do not move to produce two submarines a year as soon as possible, we are in serious danger of falling behind China, and we may have to accept dangerous risks elsewhere because we have too few submarines."

Not to worry. Thanks in large measure to Lieberman's efforts, there are plans to build as many as thirty of these submarines for a total of $75 billion, which puts them right up there on the list of super-expensive weapons for which there is no longer a demonstrable need. Nor do the submarines' irrelevance to meeting any real security threats matter. Whether we're talking about spanking-new Virginia-class submarines, F-22 and F-35 fighter jets, or V-22 Osprey tiltrotor helicopters, once the wheels are set in motion for a weapons system and profits and jobs are in play, production becomes next to impossible to stop.

But Lieberman's argument that this post-9/11 antiterrorist weapon is needed to counter the Chinese is particularly bizarre coming from a politician presumed by some of his critics to be overly influenced by the pro-Israel lobby when Israel, after

Russia, is one of the most important suppliers of sophisticated weaponry to China. If China somehow is connected with the Islamic terrorism with which Lieberman has otherwise been preoccupied, why has Israel been so supportive of China's attempts to modernize its military? According to the 2007 Annual Report to Congress, prepared by the U.S. Office of the Secretary of Defense: "Israel has also historically been a supplier of advanced military technology to China. The Israelis transferred HARPY UCAVs [Unmanned Combat Aerial Vehicles] to China in 2001 and conducted maintenance on HARPY parts during 2003–2004." While noting that, "In 2005, Israel began to improve government oversight of exports to China . . . it remains unclear to what extent the new export controls will prevent additional sensitive military-related transfers to Beijing in the future."

The passage of the sophisticated technology of UCAVs, which extend spy drones to war-fighting functions, is critical to the arms races of the future. It is generally assumed in defense circles that the current generation of manned fighters, the F-35 Raptor being the best example, will be the last, and that dominance of the skies in the future will be won through pilotless planes. The HARPY, which Israel started selling to China as early as 1994, became a major source of U.S.-Israel conflict in 2004, when U.S. intelligence determined that Israel was updating the Chinese weapons to make them even more effective in taking out radar installations. That would make the HARPY a very valuable weapon in any confrontation over the future of Taiwan, which the Defense Department report makes clear is the focus of China's increased military expenditures: "For the moment, China's military is focused on assuring the capability to prevent Taiwan independence and, if Beijing were to decide to adopt such an approach, to compel the island to negotiate a settlement on Beijing's terms. At the same time, China is laying the foundation for a force able to accomplish broader regional and global objectives." China is still a Third World military force, as the Pentagon report makes clear: "The Intelligence Community estimates China will take until the end of this decade or later to produce a modern force capable of defeating a moderate-size adversary."

There is nothing in the Defense Department survey to suggest that China could mount a threat to the United States, or that the enormous gap between the two nations will do anything but widen over the next decade. Even if one accepts the higher U.S. estimates of China's military spending, the Bush administration received more than twice that amount in supplementary funding for the 2008 budget just for Iraq and Afghanistan. The Defense Department analysis makes clear that most of China's spending is to support its massive standing army of 2.3 million troops, and that it will lag in technology far behind a score of other nations well into the future. The area of concern for Lieberman, China's navy, still does not have the capacity to build an aircraft carrier, and the sophisticated electronics for the ships they do have are mostly imported.

Despite Lieberman's alarms, China's strategic threat to the United States is a joke compared to that presented by Russia. The nuclear arsenal of China, according to Pentagon data, consists of twenty aging liquid fuel fixed silo-based CSS-4 ICBMs (Intercontinental Ballistic Missiles) that easily could be taken out were they ever moved into a launch stage. Clearly, China has not made any serious advances in strategic nuclear weapons. And there is no evidence to dispute the claim of Beijing's 2006 Defense White Paper that China "has never entered into and will never enter into a nuclear arms race with any other country," and continues to adhere to a policy of "no first use of nuclear weapons at any time and under any circumstances." That's a commitment that the United States still refuses to make, and instead is pursuing a new generation of "usable" nuclear weapons.

But the perceived threat from China has no more to do with Lieberman's support for weapons that are produced in Connecticut than does the effectiveness of those weapons in responding to the post-9/11 threat from terrorists. What it has to do with is finding an enemy, any enemy that will justify spending U.S. tax dollars on weapons produced in his home state. The threats change but the weapons remain pretty much the same—high tech, expensive, and produced primarily by the big three Connecticut defense contractors. That would be General Dynamics' Electric Boat Company, which makes submarines, and the two subsidiaries of United Technologies—Sikorsky, which manufactures helicopters, and Pratt & Whitney, whose airplane engines go into Lockheed's F-22 and F-35 Raptor fighters. For a decade before 9/11, Lieberman was fighting hard for those weapons, armed with a compelling emotional, albeit irrational, argument, repurposing old weapons to meet the new threat.

Before 9/11, Lieberman was one of the main advocates on the Senate Armed Services Committee for money for all of those Cold War legacy programs. He fought the efforts of Bush I and his defense secretary, Cheney, to cut the Seawolf submarine and obtained money under Clinton to continue production until the Virginia sub came on line.

The Gore-Lieberman presidential campaign in 2000 actually favored a more substantial military buildup than did George W. Bush, promising, in Gore's words, to "set aside more than twice as much" as Bush did for new military hardware. Bush had dared to suggest that it might not be necessary in light of the collapse of the Soviet Union to push ahead with planned new weapons like the F-22 and the F-35, costing respectively $65 billion and $300 billion, and Gore condemned him for "skipping the next generation of weapons . . . I think that's a big mistake because I think we have to stay at the cutting edge." No wonder that defense contractors warmed to the Democrats; for example, Bernard Schwartz, head of Loral Space & Communications, donated $1.1 million to the Democratic Party before the 2000 election.

After 9/11, when President Bush added $80 billion to the previous year's defense budget, he was roundly condemned by Lieberman for not spending enough. Lieberman told the *New York Times* on February 10, 2002, that Bush was only allocating $35 billion in new money in the 2003 budget and regretted deeply that there wasn't more left for new weapons:

> The president's proposed $35 billion increase dwindles substantially when you factor in inflation, critically important pay raises mandated by Congress and owed to the troops, necessary improvements to military health, and other obligations we must meet. What's left over is less than $10 billion, which is not nearly enough to meet the military's essential needs for procurement and transformation.

Quite an exaggeration, given the big winners in Connecticut: Electric Boat got a big piece of that 2003 budget, $2.5 billion for a Virginia-class sub to be built in the next fiscal year and advance payment on building yet another sub the following year. The company also was awarded another $1 billion to upgrade four older nuclear-missile-carrying submarines. Neil D. Ruenzel, spokesman for Electric Boat, was much more thankful than Lieberman had been, saying, in a *New York Times* article on February 10, 2002, "We're pleased that the president's budget recognizes the continuing need for submarines," as well he should have been, given that they had limited usefulness in preventing al Qaeda terrorists from hijacking commercial planes. And given Bush's commitment, it was only a short time later that even more subs were ordered.

Lieberman also failed to acknowledge other gifts Bush made to Connecticut contractors, such as the billions in new money for the Raptor fighters and a couple of billion more for helicopters, including the Comanche. Despite the protestations of Lieberman and his fellow Democratic Connecticut senator, Christopher Dodd, the Comanche was terminated two years later because its stealth radar-avoiding features were deemed less valuable, given the greater effectiveness of drone planes. Unfortunately, $9 billion had been wasted on the development of this helicopter, and although the manufacturers were paid some $600 million in termination fees, jobs were lost.

Sikorsky was not spoiling for a fight with the Pentagon, which had ordered more of its Blackhawk helicopters, but Lieberman expressed irritation with the company, complaining that he was even more aggressive than the defense contractor in seeking Pentagon billions. He told the *New York Times* on April 25, 2004, "Sikorsky has effectively declared itself a noncombatant here—they've accepted the decision." Not so Lieberman, who proclaimed, "We feel we have a responsibility to fight this on two grounds, national security and jobs, and we're going to do it even if Sikorsky is not with us."

For Lieberman, like other Democratic hawks, national security and money for his state seem always intertwined, and I would not hazard a guess here as to his priorities when the two conflict. One could make a strong argument that most of the money spent on the weapons systems pushed by Lieberman over the years could have served national security better if the next generation of weapons was skipped. Clearly, U.S. supremacy in the air and on the seas was fully guaranteed once the Soviets bowed out of the arms race with the last generations of weapons. When attention came to be focused on the war on terror, one could come up with a long list of non-hardware items, from Arabic translators to water purification plants, that likely would have been more effective in making the Arab world less hostile to the United States while denying the terrorists a disgruntled populace. As for jobs, there are many things for which workers can be trained other than building unneeded fighter jets and submarines.

Actually, the number of jobs from defense contracts relative to the general population tends to be small: Only about 11,000 workers in and around Groton, Connecticut, where the subs are built, appeared on the payroll financed by Defense Department funds. But those workers and managers have families, they are customers of retail stores and professional services, and the multiplier effect is substantially larger than their numbers alone indicate. Also, as Lieberman, Senator Dodd, and the state's media outlets, led by the *Hartford Courant* newspaper, often would point out, Electric Boat was only part of a defense industry that they felt was critically important to the state's economic health.

No matter what else could be done with the taxpayer dollars wasted on unnecessary weapons systems, it is money in hand. Few politicians representing constituents who benefit want to argue that defense workers, like anyone else, would gain from more rational use of the taxpayers' money, be it for better defense or job training programs for those workers. While Lieberman in part seems always to have been driven by an ideological commitment to a huge military, other politicians who do not share his worldview can be just as focused on securing defense dollars.

At the end of the day, in 2007, when the decision was made to double submarine production rather than kill the program, the key legislator was a freshman member of the House not previously known as a major hawk but who was painfully aware of the importance of those subs to the job market affecting his constituents.

Indeed, for that one congressman, those submarine-related jobs became his obsession, and when it came to working the halls of Congress to seek more funding for the program than the Pentagon asked for during the budget consideration of 2007, it was Representative Joe Courtney who saved the day. Not only did he represent the area around Groton, the self-proclaimed Submarine Capital of the World, where the sub is built, but he was a freshman congressman who had been elected to office with the slimmest margin of victory in the nation, an eighty-three vote difference out of a total of 242,413 ballots cast; his victory was determined by a painstaking recount.

Courtney is a progressive Democrat closer to Dodd, whom he represented as a surrogate during the 2008 presidential primaries, than to Lieberman, who had been reelected to his Senate seat as an Independent after being rejected by the voters in the state's Democratic primary. During Courtney's own grueling campaign for his hotly contested 2006 House seat, he had been castigated by incumbent Republican Rob Simmons as not to be trusted to deliver the defense dollar. The sharpies in Congress would snatch defense jobs from Courtney "like candy from a baby," Simmons's ads had threatened. After Courtney won, the Republicans recruited a retired Navy captain who was a former commander of the submarine base in Groton to be his next opponent.

So, clearly, Courtney wanted more submarines, and the Democratic leaders in Congress who after the 2006 election owed their control of the House to freshmen like Courtney were eager to help out. Courtney's goal was to get $588 million more for the sub program than the Pentagon had requested in order to commit the government to producing two subs a year rather than the one that had been agreed to only after the intervention of Lieberman and others. He was the new kid on the congressional block, and as the *Hartford Courant*, the state's leading newspaper and editorially a cheerleader for the submarine program, put it in a news story November 14, 2007, in praising Courtney:

> He started work on the submarine funding during his first moments in office, shepherding the $588 million as it wound through the long budget process. He secured a hearing on the issue before the House's seapower committee. He courted a powerful ally, U.S. Rep. Jack Murtha, D-Pa., who agreed to visit Electric Boat. He wrote letters and whispered in ears. On the Senate side, Senators Christopher Dodd and Joseph Lieberman pushed a similar though lesser amount.

As a result of their strenuous efforts and the desire of the Democratic leadership to make a very insecure congressional seat more secure, the money was appropriated, and the nation was on its way to building two submarines a year at $2.5 billion apiece (the 2008 budget increased it to $3.1 billion) when there was no compelling need for even one.

Calling it "pork" pure and simple, Ivan Eland, a former defense analyst at the Congressional Budget Office and now a senior fellow at the watchdog Independent Institute, accepted that "A submarine is probably the most powerful naval weapon ever created." But, he added in an interview in the November 14, 2007, *Hartford Courant*, "The problem is, we don't really have an enemy right now."

Attempts to use the enemy of the moment, Islamic terrorists, to justify a deep-sea underwater fighting vessel is absurd on its face, although efforts were made to assign an intelligence-gathering role to the sub in intercepting communications. In making the case for the sub and other needed weapons for which he found increased funding, Courtney invoked the same one that Lieberman had used—China—and he threw in Cold War enemy Russia for good measure.

After chortling happily, once funding was secured, about the jobs saved and presumably the voters' support earned, he said, "I'm ecstatic," adding that it was a "great day for southeastern Connecticut." But in case one wondered why we couldn't just pay those workers to stay home or train for a new occupation without also building submarines, Courtney fell back on the tried-and-true obligation to protect national security: "The world is changing. We're seeing the country of Russia rebounding economically and correspondingly increasing the size of their army and their navy. And China is the other real maritime power out there we need to respond to."

Just gibberish. We still had a substantial fleet of submarines that had been more than a match for the old Soviet Union and which could certainly handle the now decrepit Russian subs if their commanders would allow them to submerge for any length of time. As for China's submarine threat, defense budget expert Eland said it best: "The Chinese submarines are all junk. There's no national security issue here."

But that didn't stop Connecticut's leading newspaper on

November 16, 2007, from applauding Courtney's success and endorsing his national security claim: "A healthy submarine industry in Connecticut is good for the State's economy and the nation's defense," editorialized the *Hartford Courant*, which gloated, "After a rough two years, Connecticut can boast that it is back in the saddle of the submarine-building business."

No doubt Courtney will be able to count on the paper's endorsement in his next campaign, for as the paper editorialized in a booster tone quite typical of local media's treatment of defense contracts throughout the country:

> Considering that the Pentagon had tried (and failed) only two years ago to close the Groton submarine base, expanding the submarine program represents quite a victory for the state's congressional delegation. Give much of the credit to Rep. Joe Courtney, whose district includes the Groton submarine base and who inserted the $588 million request in the bill. Rep. John Murtha of Pennsylvania, the chairman of the House defense appropriations subcommittee, has stood in Connecticut's corner. He passed the bill with Mr. Courtney's request intact.

Murtha is the king of defense pork, the master of the earmark, and it is odd that a newspaper would so crassly celebrate his throwing some Connecticut's way. The *Hartford Courant*, then owned by the Tribune Company, is a respected newspaper, which makes all the more appalling its brazen celebration of a defense expenditure that now could be expected to grow to at least $5 billion a year for two submarines the Pentagon did not want but which was good for "Connecticut's corner." But it is no different from the coverage of such spending by newspapers and television stations across the country, which treat defense spending as local jobs-and-profit programs.

Of course, the *Courant* repeated the phony national security claim for the subs: "The submarine fleet, considered a crucial component of the nation's military forces, will be able to maintain a competitive edge over those of Russia and China and others." The newspaper ignored the obvious question: If it was such a crucial component, why did the Pentagon try to kill it? The invocation of an enemy, while transparent as a means of grabbing defense dollars for Connecticut, is also insidious in its ability to stoke an arms race.

It is the same language used by Murtha in supporting not just the Virginia-class sub but other Cold War relic weapons as well, particularly the F-22 fighter, a plane that was supposed to be winding down when we had the 183 that the Pentagon had asked for and Congress had authorized. But Murtha found another $3.15 billion for the 2008 budget to buy twenty more F-22s, "because of what's happening in China."

Now most of us would think that what's happening in China is that they are busily producing consumer goods. As opposed to some, like Lieberman, Murtha was hesitant to predict that China would become an enemy: "I'm not saying that they will be a threat to the United States, but we have to be prepared." For the Martians as well.

Just so we understand how nutty this all is, the United States entered this century as the world's sole superpower, possessing an armed force more than equal to handling a naval or air war challenge not just from China but from the entire world's military, friend and foe, combined. Since that time, we have spent more money modernizing our military than that expended by all of those other nations together. Yet, and with a straight face, the Liebermans and Murthas dare tell us that our security depends on an even more rapid buildup. They have no shame.

As for that eager-beaver freshman congressman, Courtney, he is well on his way to becoming another Lieberman or Dodd as he scoops up defense industry dollars and ensures his future reelection. The unionized workers on the sub greeted him as a conquering hero when he visited their union hall, and the company execs couldn't have been more pleased. "Remember?" Courtney asked the workers in the union hall, parodying his defeated opponent's negative television ads, "No clout. No military experience. They'll take defense jobs like candy from a baby."

The workers cheered the fact that Courtney had delivered more money than his Republican predecessor, and one shouted, "Joe for president." Courtney then left for a tour of Electric Boat, where he met with company president John P. Casey, who had supported his opponent. This time around, things were different; Courtney had the backing of the Democratic majority in Congress and delivered the goods, so Casey had responded with a personal $1,000 contribution to Courtney's reelection, and others at the company already had come up with an additional eighteen grand. It was just the beginning of great things. Courtney promised even newer and more expensive subs to be built in the future: "The next step is to continue discussions for increasing design work on the next-generation submarine." I have gone on so long about Courtney as the obvious heir to Lieberman to indicate that it may be as obvious a motive as political ambition that drives this madness.

When it comes to politicians most fervently supporting the defense contractors, the common denominator is not religion, political ideology, ethnic background, or political party affiliation. It is rather, as Eisenhower warned, whether the tentacles of the military-industrial complex, those lucrative job-creating and campaign-contribution-generating defense contractors, happen to be located in their constituency. A new sub, for example, can help Lieberman get reelected, even as an Independent.

But at what price? Lieberman is a hawk in the Henry "Scoop" Jackson Cold War–liberal mold who long has believed in combining a pro-defense posture with strong support for spending on domestic social programs. It is a guns-and-butter approach that failed Jackson and the president he supported, Lyndon Baines Johnson, when they witnessed the sacrifice of their War on Poverty to the real war in Vietnam. It is true that many Democrats like Lieberman, Dodd, Murtha, and Courtney believe that military expenditures represent a jobs program and so do not feel conflicted that they are wasting money that could be put to better use.

That bubble burst on November 13 when George Bush signed the defense appropriation, including the money for the sub, into law. That spending authorization for $459 billion represented a $40 billion increase over the previous year—and that's without counting the almost $200 billion in additional funding for the Iraq and Afghanistan wars that the president demanded and Lieberman supported.

Yet the same day that he approved the immense Defense Department budget, the largest since World War II in real dollars when the war costs are added in, Bush vetoed the budget law passed by Congress covering the departments of Labor, Health and Human Services, and Education. Bush wanted a $4 billion cut in the previous year's allotment, and the Democrats had added $10 billion in spending.

No matter that Bush had added $40 billion to the total for the military, a 9.5 percent increase that dwarfed the 4.3 percent hike in the domestic budget for health, hunger, and education needs of its people. The president blasted the Democrats for their "tax and spend" policies in a statement November 13, 2007: "The majority was elected on a pledge of fiscal responsibility, but so far it's acting like a teenager with a new credit card. This year alone, the leadership in Congress has proposed to spend $22 billion more than my budget provides. Now, some of them claim that's not really much of a difference—the scary part is, they seem to mean it."

Even overlooking Bush's questionable accuracy on the $22 billion difference, it does seem not that great an amount compared to throwing almost $200 billion down the rat hole of Iraq, or $65 billion for the F-22 program, and a whopping $300 billion for the F-35 joint fighter. But such comparisons are obviously beside the point because Bush claimed that the domestic spending bill was laden with earmarks "such as a prison museum, a sailing school taught aboard a catamaran, and a program teaching Portuguese as a second language."

Nothing wasteful like that could ever happen with the military appropriation. Nope, those billions for yet another submarine were absolutely needed. It's an argument, this guns versus butter issue, that goes back at least as far as biblical scripture, and that can never be won by those who want both plowshares and at the same time an excess of swords.

The delusion of the Democrats is twofold: Military expenditures can be used for meaningful social programs such as job training through the military, and even if the money is totally wasted there will be enough left over to fund more needed domestic programs. Democrats, certainly since the failed presidential campaign of George McGovern, have been wary of being "soft on defense" and have come to regard the reform of military expenditures as a politically life-threatening third rail.

Being as irrational as hawkish Republicans in support of a bloated defense budget was a hallmark of Cold War liberals such as Lieberman. With the demise of the Soviet Union, that support for a huge military came to be justified by a new breed of neoliberals who cited a U.S. obligation to militarily intervene internationally, ostensibly in protection of human rights.

Chapter 8

YES, VIRGINIA, THERE ARE LIBERAL HAWKS

Much is made of the role of the neoconservatives in resurrecting the militaristic globalism of the Cold War, and the reach of this small band of ideologues has been decisive. However, they could not have done it alone, given the political party structure in the United States, were it not for the active support of a group carrying an apparently opposite label—neoliberals—but possessed of a roughly common purpose.

Both groups called for the ramped-up use of the U.S. military in response to post–Cold War problems, and both embraced a vision of a benighted American empire liberating the world from its travails. But whereas the neocons worked the Republican side of the street, the neoliberals represented the hawkish side of the Democratic Party. Key in this camp is Richard Holbrooke, a Democratic veteran of the Cold War going back to the Vietnam era, Clinton's U.N. Ambassador, a backer of the U.S. invasion of Iraq, and more recently a key foreign policy adviser to Hillary Clinton.

Holbrooke, as was typical of the neolibs, fully endorsed the neocon call for war in Iraq: "Now it's time to use an approach that builds on the fact that Saddam is the most dangerous government leader in the world today, he poses a threat to the region, he could pose a larger threat if he got weapons of mass destruction deployed, and we have a legitimate right to take action," Holbrooke said in an interview with Chris Matthews, on January 23, 2003. He added, "The American public always supports its commander in chief, and we unify in times of crisis, and if the action is fast and rapid and successful, afterwards everyone will think they supported it." If not, then folks like Holbrooke will just as sanguinely criticize the result of invasion as the "worst foreign policy disaster since the Vietnam War," as he did seven months later, on August 26, 2003. In an interview with the daily *Berliner Zeitung*, Holbrooke blamed the disastrous Iraq occupation on poor planning. "They [Americans] could not predict the nature of this war," Holbrooke said. Of course, Holbrooke failed to predict it himself.

Holbrooke's reference to Vietnam, a war initiated by the still-revered Democratic President John F. Kennedy and vastly accelerated by another Democrat, Lyndon Johnson, illustrates the reality that foreign adventurism has been a bipartisan avocation. Yet having participated in the Vietnam debacle of the Johnson administration did not cause Holbrooke to bridle his initial enthusiasm for the invasion of Iraq.

Let me confess to having had one very unpleasant encounter with Holbrooke relating to the aftermath of the Vietnam War that is worth recounting because it reveals much of the double standard on human rights that informs the foreign policy claims of the neoliberals. The occasion, in 1979, was a small dinner party of about eight people at the Los Angeles home of television producer Norman Lear, at which Holbrooke and sixties folksinger Joan Baez were the guests of honor. They had just returned from a trip to Thailand in the company of First Lady Rosalynn Carter and were bubbling with enthusiasm for a coalition of Cambodian exiles formed in 1979 to overthrow the Vietnamese-backed government in Phnom Penh that had routed the genocidal Pol Pot regime. Holbrooke was assistant secretary of state for East Asian and Pacific affairs in the Carter administration, which was supporting the Cambodian exile coalition. The only problem, as I insisted on pointing out at the dinner, was that the coalition included the bloody butcher Pol Pot and his Khmer Rouge army.

This was after Pol Pot had committed his genocide, killing at least a million Cambodians, for such crimes as wearing glasses, as well as many Vietnamese living along the border of the two countries. Finally the Vietnamese had intervened, and in the wake of their successful invasion, they had installed a Cambodian ally, Hun Sen, in power. The human rights implications were clear, and from that point of view, the Vietnamese had done the right thing, but the wounds of the U.S. defeat in the war with that country were still raw, and the Carter administration seized upon this as a way to show resolution. It also allowed the United States to cozy up to the Chinese communists, who were at odds with the Soviets and backers of Pol Pot. To its everlasting shame, the U.S. under President Carter and then Reagan, supported the exiled Pol Pot group in keeping its seat at the United Nations. The perpetrators of one of the world's gravest genocides were thus legitimatized as representatives of the Cambodian people.

The fact that Holbrooke embraced such a strategy tells a great deal about the neoliberal mind-set: Human rights violations only occur on someone else's watch. Neoliberals insist most of all that foreign policy be prohuman rights, but rarely does that translate into concern about human rights violations committed by their own government, and certainly not those of an administration that employs them. Holbrooke, for example, has never referred to the carpet bombing and other attacks on Indochina as genocidal. Yet that war, in which former Secretary of Defense Robert McNamara concedes 3.4 million Indochinese died, could not then or now be justified as having any logical connection with U.S. national security issues. (In a rather bizarre plan to further the cause of human rights in the Balkans, in 1995 Holbrooke reportedly favored NATO dropping "bombs for peace" on Bosnia as a way to pressure Bosnian Serb leader Slobodan Milošević to negotiate.)

What is forgotten is that the original arguments for intervening in Vietnam, back in those earlier Democratic administrations, often relied on mixing human rights concerns with those of U.S. national security. The argument made for the first covert installment of American troops, cleverly called "flood control advisers," sent by President John F. Kennedy in support of South Vietnam's ruler, Ngo Dinh Diem, centered on the threat allegedly represented to the freedom of the Vietnamese people living in the south by the communist-run north and its surrogates in the south, the Vietcong insurgents.

The "protect freedom" argument always rang hollow, given that Ngo Dinh Diem, who had been residing in a Catholic seminary in New Jersey in 1954 when Ho Chi Minh's revolutionaries defeated the French colonialists, had been installed in power in the south by the United States. Elections called for in the peace agreement signed between the French and Ho Chi Minh to unify the country were never allowed by the U.S. to proceed, and instead, a myth of a democratic Vietnam based in the south was built around Diem.

Unfortunately, Diem, a Catholic, was not accepted by his

countrymen, 90 percent of whom were Buddhist, and his image as a free-world leader dissolved when Buddhist monks began immolating themselves to protest his regime. Diem, who had been dubbed by his American backers "the George Washington of Vietnam"—it was great PR—was unceremoniously deposed and killed in a coup supported by the Kennedy administration. Yet while puppet governments subsequently came and went at the pleasure of the Americans in charge, the self-determination of the Vietnamese people continued as a justification for the U.S. occupation.

It is important to recall that bit of history, for it was repeated in Iraq, where first Ahmed Chalabi, dubbed by some "the George Washington of Iraq," and then Iyad Allawi were similarly presented as great liberators of their people. Both had been handpicked by the United States, and both turned out to have little support or other connection to the Iraqi people. Chalabi, the Iraqi exile and fugitive from Jordan, influenced the Clinton administration to sign off on the Iraq Liberation Act he was pushing; later, the Bush administration invaded the country in part at his behest. While wildly popular with U.S. government leaders, Chalabi received less than 1 percent of the vote in the much-ballyhooed Iraqi election.

Another thread that runs from the Vietnam disaster to the Iraq debacle for the war faction in the Democratic Party is its claim of access to information that the skeptics, and of course the general public, does not have. In supporting the Iraq invasion, Holbrooke used his experience in the Clinton administration to back his claim that Saddam threatened U.S. security with the ability to deploy weapons of mass destruction. Of course, one could counter that claim by asking: If the evidence was so clear that Saddam's WMD threatened America, why didn't the Clinton administration invade?

Since neither Holbrooke nor any other Clinton administration veteran claimed knowledge of a connection between
Saddam and bin Laden, the 9/11 attacks would hardly provide
a justification for changing the Clinton posture of containing,
rather than eliminating, Saddam. Yet that did not stop Clinton's
National Security Council adviser Sandy Berger from seizing
upon 9/11 as an excuse to support the Iraq invasion: "The urgency of this really changes when you link Saddam Hussein and
terrorism," Berger said in an interview with Chris Matthews,
on February 13, 2003. "I think after 9/11, the risk of not acting
tends to be seen as more compelling than the risk of acting."
Berger, having had access to the same data viewed by Richard
Clarke, the top terrorism expert in both the Clinton and Bush
administrations, whose memoir demolishes the case for the Iraq
War, knew full well that there was no connection between
Saddam and the 9/11 terrorists. In short, he had parlayed his
insider status to all the more effectively deceive the public into
supporting the war.

An even more blatant example of misusing access to secret
information was provided by another veteran of the Clinton
administration who lobbied most vociferously for taking out
Saddam Hussein. In the lead-up to the U.S. invasion of Iraq, no
Democratic policy expert was more effective in championing
the war than Kenneth M. Pollack, whose book *The Threatening
Storm: The Case for Invading Iraq*, published in September 2002,
became the bible of pro-war Democrats. Pollack, who was on
Clinton's National Security Council, and Martin S. Indyk, his
colleague at the Democratic-leaning Brookings Institution and
Clinton's ambassador to Israel, wrote a very influential *Los Angeles Times* column December 19, 2002, in which they played
the insider card to its full advantage.

"As former U.S. government officials who had access to the

most sensitive U.S. intelligence on Iraq, we are well aware of Iraq's continued efforts to retain and enhance its weapons capabilities," they wrote. Pollack and Indyk were fully confident that the weapons existed, including "Thousands of tons of precursor chemicals for chemical warfare agents, thousands of liters of biological warfare agents . . ." that remain unaccounted for. They argued with total confidence that the United Nations inspectors on the ground lacked the will and competency to find those and other weapons: "Chief U.N. weapons inspector Hans Blix and International Atomic Energy Agency Director General Mohamed [El] Baradei have repeatedly resisted U.S. efforts to direct their activities and demurred from exercising the more aggressive powers that the U.N. resolution allows them because their interest lies in encouraging Iraqi cooperation, not serving as the trigger for a war."

Horrors—those U.N. officials would not make acting as a trigger for war their highest priority. But the reality, as we discovered after the invasion, is that the inspectors had done an excellent job and, indeed, the aforementioned El Baradei and the agency he heads received the Nobel Peace Prize for their efforts.

One has to question if Pollack and Indyk, their own itchy trigger fingers at the keyboard, were interested in the truth concerning WMD or simply determined to make the case for war. They began their article with the flat-out declaratory statement, "Saddam Hussein has failed to come clean. His denial of possessing any weapons of mass destruction makes that clear, even though the experts have not completed their review of Iraq's weapons declaration."

But ironically it was Pollack and Indyk who failed to "come clean" as to how they, with their access to "sensitive U.S. intelligence on Iraq," got it wrong in disparaging the work of the United Nations inspectors on the ground. They wrote:

Moreover, neither the U.S. intelligence community nor the inspectors have or are likely to come into possession of the necessary intelligence that would uncover Iraq's prohibited weaponry or production facilities. . . . We have plenty of intelligence that Iraq has prohibited items, but no reliable indications of where they are hidden. Spiriting Iraqi scientists out of the country might help, but some are likely to be missing, others unwilling to leave, and the rest might fear for loved ones left behind.

After the invasion, many of those Iraqi scientists were arrested, and they and others were certainly no longer concerned about the safety of their loved ones from the wrath of Saddam Hussein. But it turns out that they had been telling the truth. What is the excuse for Pollack and Indyk to insist upon the existence of "plenty of intelligence that Iraq has prohibited items," when they must have known from their insider status in the Clinton administration exactly how flimsy the argument for war was? In their case, one assumes they perpetuated this myth not out of any fear for their personal safety from the U.S. government, but rather, as they have indicated in their other writings, out of a reasoning that some larger noble end, like bringing democracy to Iraq or creating a better neighborhood for Israel, justified the means of dissembling fact and logic.

Indeed, the truth was the obstacle rather than the means to a desirable policy: "There is real risk in allowing the inspections to run on indefinitely. The longer the inspections go on and find nothing, the harder it will be for the U.S. to build a coalition when we finally decide to take action."

Ponder that sentence if you will, for it fully expresses the contempt for fact and logic that so often underlies the case for war. More frightening is the ease with which such deception can prove effective even in a society that prides itself on the checks and balances explicit in the U.S. Constitution. It is further evidence, not that any should be needed, of the incompatibility of empire building with democracy, for the misuse of classified data by proponents of the agenda of the national security state is just too wickedly effective.

In the consideration of domestic policy, shorn as it is of the protective mantle of national security, there is no necessity for secrecy or rather for classification of the key information that ends in a mockery of democratic decision making. It would be exceptional, indeed blatantly ludicrous, for officials to claim that they cannot share with the public the basic data behind the decision to build a new school, permit spraying a field crop, or change the age of Social Security retirement. But if you want to invade Iraq, Democrats and Republicans alike find it all too easy to choose whichever facts serve their cause, with little regard to the larger truth.

Take the example of George Tenet, a veteran of the Clinton administration who went to work for Bush II. After retiring as head of the CIA, Tenet was granted the Medal of Freedom by Bush as a reward for eagerly lending the credibility of the CIA to the administration's distortions. In the first paragraph of Chapter 17 of his memoir, *At the Center of the Storm: My Years at the CIA*, Tenet states: "The United States did not go to war in Iraq solely because of WMD. In my view, I doubt it was even the principal cause. Yet it was the public face that was put on it."

Quite a clever formulation that is, for turning a betrayal of Congress and public into an acceptable tactical device in the interest of democratic governance. As was just indicated, the public was told by leading Democrats with access to classified material that war was necessary because of the pressing threat of Saddam Hussein's WMD, and here the top intelligence figure in both the Clinton and Bush administrations concedes that it was merely a tactic to garner support for a policy that the public might otherwise reject. As Tenet put it,

> The leaders of a country decide to go to war because of core beliefs, larger geostrategic calculations, ideology, and, in the case of Iraq, because of the administration's largely unarticulated view that the democratic transformation of the Middle East through regime change in Iraq would be worth the price. WMD was, as Paul Wolfowitz was quoted as saying in *Vanity Fair* in May 2003, something that "we settled on" because it was "the one issue that everyone could agree on."

It is odd that Tenet appears not the least bit embarrassed championing the "democratic transformation of the Middle East" while conceding that the explicit price of moving toward that goal was the sacrifice of the most obvious requirement of democratic rule at home: decision making by an informed public. The very idea that this country's leaders can decide to go to war on the basis of their "core beliefs" which they leave "unarticulated" while frightening the public with exaggerated claims makes a mockery of the notion of self-governance. Some would consider it an offense worthy of impeachment. As a tactic, panicking the citizenry with the phantom of Saddam's WMD in the hands of 9/11-type terrorists is no different from Adolf Hitler blaming international Jewry and foreign communists for the Reichstag fire. The fact that Hitler was scaremongering to win a free election hardly qualifies as an advertisement for democracy.

The Hitler analogy will of course rankle most readers because our leaders have not come close to such levels of barbarism. I inserted it, though, having just reread Kenneth Pollack's book *The Threatening Storm* in which he, as did many of the proponents of this preemptive war, compares the menace of Saddam Hussein to that once posed by Hitler. Pollack made the case that invading Iraq

> in the near term, when Saddam has only a limited stockpile of weapons of mass destruction and his conventional forces remain weak, is likely to seem effortless and cost-free compared to a war with Saddam after he has crossed the nuclear threshold. . . . The moment we face is reminiscent of another in early 1938. At that time, France and Britain were unquestionably stronger than Nazi Germany. They looked out across the Rhine and saw a Germany they knew would trouble them in the future. They saw in Adolf Hitler a leader who was aggressive, willing to use force, and rapidly rebuilding Germany's strength. . . . Just as France and Britain should have taken up arms in 1938, I believe that the United States should take up arms against Iraq to end the threat from Saddam Hussein's regime once and for all.

Pollack had the advantage of working seven years as a CIA Iran-Iraq military analyst and inside Clinton's National Security Council for three more. He had to know what the public now knows, that Saddam was a hobbled dictator who had neither a

WMD program nor the means to create one in the foreseeable future. Aerial surveillance of Iraq, intercession on the high seas, the witness of opposition elements, and the presence of U.N. inspectors all made it quite obvious that the comparison of the threat of Saddam with that of Hitler at the helm of one of the best educated and most industrially advanced nations in the world was absurd. The notion that we didn't even have a year to allow the inspectors to complete their work was simply a vicious and irresponsible fraud—vicious, because Pollack was playing with fears made raw in the wake of 9/11, and as a Democrat, he did as much as any neocon fanatic to cheerlead this nation into a war that he later would acknowledge had disastrous outcomes.

This point deserves to be stressed: The rush to war with Iraq was a bipartisan affair, and as we have witnessed repeatedly in the postwar period, deceit in the pursuit of militarism is an all too easily rewarded stance. Were that not the case, the leading proponents of the Iraq war would not have appeared so numerously among the ranks of foreign policy advisers to the top candidates of both parties in the run-up to the 2008 presidential election. Nor would it be so lacking in inconvenience to one's career as a public pundit to have been so egregiously wrong.

After the fact, leading Democrats—including Hillary Clinton and John Kerry, senators who voted to authorize Bush to go to war—claimed that they didn't really intend that outcome and instead trusted that the president would use their votes as a bargaining tool to get Saddam to comply with the United Nations. Or they argue that they based their vote on faulty intelligence supplied by the Republican administration, which cherry-picked the data. These are nonsensical rationalizations for politicians in possession of high-security clearances and with access to enough data to know that the arguments for the invasion were false. Yet they went along.

Why they did is not so difficult to explain in terms of career advancement, political opportunism, and ideological orientation. On the Democratic side, there always has been a strong pull to appear tough in foreign policy because of the historic advantage enjoyed by Republicans after the McCarthyism smears against the loyalty of high-ranking Democrats. As Democratic candidates move from the primary season, where the peace movement has some strength, to the general election, they have come to expect that proving their patriotic bona fides is critical to winning more conservative votes. Toward that end, with brief exceptions like the 1972 campaign of George McGovern, a much decorated pilot from World War II, and a winner of the Distinguished Flying Cross, who was blasted by Navy noncombatant Richard Nixon for being a wimp, the Democrats have been loath to exhibit integrity in the policy area, where, as a matter of life and death, it is most compellingly important.

Up to this point, I have treated the motives of the pro-war liberals on their own terms, according to the human rights concerns that they claim motivate them. But there are, as with the neocons, also career and financial gains that accrue from assuming a more hawkish stance. The military-industrial lobby has long had strong support on the Democratic side of the aisle, which was quite supportive of previous war efforts and military buildups, both under Harry Truman during the first years of the Cold War and the Kennedy and Johnson administrations during the Vietnam War.

Quite a few of the neocons now associated with the Republican Party started out working for Democrats, most notably Richard Perle. A different trajectory was followed by another "Scoop" Jackson staff member, Madeleine Albright, who stayed on the Democratic side and became Clinton's secretary of state. But Albright, while certainly not as hawkish as Perle, prides herself on a tough posture on deploying military force.

That posture was described by Colin Powell in his book *My American Journey*, when he recounted his efforts as chairman of the Joint Chiefs of Staff to caution the new Clinton administration to exercise restraint in bombing Bosnia or committing military forces there "until we had a clear political objective." Powell said a frustrated Albright, then U.N. ambassador, replied with a line that has marked the neolibs' exasperation with those who urge such restraint: "What's the point of having this superb military that you're always talking about if we can't use it?" A shocked Powell wrote, "I thought I would have an aneurysm. American GIs were not toy soldiers to be moved around on some sort of global game board." Albright had enthusiastically supported the use of massive firepower in Vietnam, as had Powell, who fought in that war. But, as opposed to the general, she does not seem to have grasped that the use of military power crosses a line that should be treated with far greater respect than her attitude indicated.

Certainly the ease with which the Clinton administration engaged in bombing the former Yugoslavia as well as Iraq in the name of humanitarian goals might give one pause. However, I would not too hastily put Albright in the category of military hawk, and in her actions in the Clinton administration she was clearly an advocate of international consultation and maximizing diplomatic options before employing the military. Certainly her gutsy efforts at negotiating an end to North Korea's nuclear program by visiting Pyongyang were an important effort at giving peace a chance. Despite harsh criticism of that effort by the Bush campaign and ensuing administration, the belated but successful renewal of diplomacy with North Korea by Bush II paid big dividends.

One is less confident about those who served under Albright and later followed her into the ranks of Hillary Clinton's campaign. By way of illustration, there is Lee Feinstein, who was deputy director of the Clinton State Department's policy planning staff, worked in the John Kerry 2004 presidential campaign, and was named Hillary Clinton's national security director in her run for the presidency. Feinstein is typical of those Washington policy experts whose careers advance in direct proportion to the errors made in their foreign policy analysis. He was picked to advise both Kerry and Hillary Clinton after he got the Iraq war all wrong, insisting in the debate before the invasion that Saddam Hussein not only possessed WMD but also that the U.N. inspectors could not be trusted to find them.

Even a month after the invasion, when it was obvious to most informed observers that the weapons were not there, Feinstein said, "I believe they will find weapons of mass destruction," although by then he had renewed respect for the U.N. inspectors and thought they should be invited in to help the United States find the missing WMD.

Feinstein signed onto a "bipartisan" statement of support for the invasion of Iraq but one that involved as much European support as possible. That Second Statement on Post-War Iraq, as it was titled, was issued by the Project for the New American Century, and the signers included a who's who of neoconservatives—William Kristol, Bruce P. Jackson, and Thomas Donnelly, among others—as well as neoliberals connected with the Democrats, such as Michael O'Hanlon, Dennis Ross, Peter Galbraith, and Martin Indyk. Most of the neolibs, like Feinstein, who also signed the statement, were veterans of the Clinton administration.

That statement solicited by Kristol was issued on March 28, 2003, and stressed the WMD issue, urging that "NATO should actively support efforts to secure and destroy all of Iraq's weapons of mass destruction stockpiles and production facilities." We all make mistakes, but taking a nation to war on the basis of what later investigation showed was a cooked-up alarmist case about the Iraq WMD threat should have provoked some soul-searching on the part of experts who had gotten it so wrong. In particular, it raises profoundly disturbing questions about the functioning of our democracy, as well as about the failure of the Democratic party in Congress and the free media to seriously question the government's claims. No such examination from the neoconservatives or the neoliberals—or the media—has been forthcoming or any doubt expressed about their own qualification to champion the cause of democracy.

In the bipartisan neocon-neolib statement there is a strong demand to reconstitute Iraq along such "democratic" lines:

> There should be no question of our common determination to help the Iraqi people establish a peaceful, stable, united, prosperous, and democratic Iraq free of weapons of mass destruction. We must help build an Iraq that is governed by a pluralistic system representative of all Iraqis and fully committed to the rule of law, the rights of all of its citizens, and the betterment of all its people. Such an Iraq will be a force for regional stability rather than conflict and participate in the democratic development of the region.

But what sort of advertisement did the United States, and those who supported an invasion based on misinformation they helped spread, provide for the Iraqis or anyone else about the vitality of democracy, the separation of powers, and the rule of law? As the Bush administration went about beating the drums for war against Iraq, the Pew Research Center for the People &

the Press, in collaboration with the Council on Foreign Relations, conducted a poll in September of 2002 on the attitudes of Americans toward an invasion. Feinstein, the Clinton adviser, then a senior fellow at the Council on Foreign Relations, wrote the commentary that accompanied the Pew report, in which he stated that "a large majority of those surveyed believe Saddam is on the threshold of having a nuclear weapons capability. Two-thirds of those surveyed (65%) say they believe Saddam is 'close to having' nuclear weapons, and 14% believe he 'already has' them." In his commentary, Feinstein noted,

> A recently released report of the CIA, although far from reassuring, indicates Saddam may still have some distance to travel. It says Iraq now lacks the weapons-grade material for a nuclear bomb; is "unlikely" to produce enough weapons-grade materials for a nuclear bomb "until the last half of the decade"; but could produce a nuclear weapon "within a year" if it could find "fissile material from abroad."

So, too, could just about every other nation in the world, for that matter. But what Feinstein misses is that the public barely knew of the CIA disclaimer at a time when the president and his cheerleaders among the neocons and neolibs were going on endlessly about weapons of mass destruction and the "smoking-gun-becomes-the-mushroom-cloud" specter employed by Condoleezza Rice, Dick Cheney, and the president himself.

Despite the claims of our free society, it turned out that it was surprisingly easy to convince the public of the administration's erroneous line. This was even more depressingly true with regard to the other major justification for the invasion—the claim of ties between Saddam Hussein and al Qaeda. As Feinstein wrote, "The Pew results indicate that the imputation of an Iraq-9/11 link strongly resonates with a majority of Americans, even though most analysts inside and outside government have disputed the suggestion of a direct link, and earlier suggestions by administration officials asserting such a link have been muted. Two-thirds of those surveyed (66%) say they believe 'Saddam Hussein helped the terrorists in the September 11 attacks.'" Two-thirds of Americans believed the deception foisted on them by the administration—good work by the spin-meisters.

There was nothing "muted" about the administration's imputation of an Iraq-9/11 link, even though it became particularly embarrassing to assert later, after the release of the 9/11 Commission Report, that there never was a shred of credible evidence to support such a connection. On the contrary, the religious fanatic bin Laden and the secular dictator Saddam were implacable enemies. The public's ignorance concerning the two main reasons offered by the administration for the war is far less a reflection on the people themselves than on the experts in and out of government, such as Lee Feinstein, who misinformed them.

This matter of an "informed public," or rather the absence of one, is all-important in considering the larger agenda of the neoliberals, who will have considerable influence in a future Democratic administration. They believe strongly in the case for U.S. military intervention based on the principle, as Feinstein asserted in an article he cowrote with Anne-Marie Slaughter in 2004, that "members of the human rights and humanitarian protection communities" have an obligation to ignore the restraint of national boundaries in order to confront "humanitarian catastrophes."

That was published in the January/February 2004 issue of

Foreign Affairs, the magazine of the Council on Foreign Relations, and it is a sign of arrogance that Feinstein would, even that late in the day, use Iraq and its nonexistent WMD as an illustration of what he had in mind, that "the world cannot afford to look the other way when faced with the prospect, as in Iraq, of a brutal ruler acquiring nuclear weapons or other weapons of mass destruction (WMD)."

The neolibs, no more than their neocon sparring partners, are not inclined to learn from past mistakes. It is discouraging that in the fall of 2007, leading Democratic candidate Hillary Clinton drew upon the advice of the very same "experts" who had talked her and other Democratic politicians into supporting the Iraq invasion. Hillary continued to rely on the advice of the very same neolibs who had previously justified the war while she pointedly argued that the invasion had weakened America's position in the world.

In an article published October 17, 2007, in the November/December issue of *Foreign Affairs*, Clinton wrote: "We had a historic opportunity to build a broad global coalition to combat terror, increase the impact of our diplomacy, and create a world with more partners and fewer adversaries. . . . But we lost that opportunity by refusing to let the U.N. inspectors finish their work in Iraq and rushing to war instead."

Fair enough—and it is also likely that the neolibs around Clinton, as opposed to the neocons who informed Bush, would favor a more cautious and multinational approach to military invasion. But that begs the question of how the "we" to whom Clinton referred gets its information. Assuming that the "we" in a representative democracy includes the public at large and not only the representatives they elect, the process is a charade if the public is systematically misinformed by those who have the time and the knowledge base to inform them accurately. The lesson of the war on terror is that when the nation is frightened by foreign enemies, and the response to the danger must be based on information that is classified and only available to political leaders, "we" the public can all too easily be betrayed by the experts, be they neoconservative or neoliberal.

Chapter 9

THE PORNOGRAPHY OF POWER

What about those weapons of mass destruction? The most frightening aspect of the 9/11 attacks for Americans was the recognition of their vulnerability to the awesome death-dispensing capacity of modern technology, a subject in which some others in the world tend to be better versed.

In this case, horror wasn't the result of a single bomb, like those first nukes we cutely named Fat Man and Little Boy, designed by the most brilliant of scientific minds to instantly implode the eyeballs and melt the skin of hundreds of thousands of innocents in Hiroshima and Nagasaki. But we did gain a slight inkling of what it might feel like to be on the receiving end of a big one. If a commercial plane flown into a tall building could have the impact it did, what would a nuclear weapon with the power to level Manhattan be like?

The attacks were all the more terrifying and confusing, given tactics that spanned five millennia of the art of violence, from crude weapons available in the Bronze Age to the use of modern commercial jet aircraft as mass-death-inducing bombs. That the terrorists were the disciples of a cave-dwelling religious fanatic inspired by orders from his supreme being rather than military professionals trained to unleash weapons of mass destruction on the instructions of their supreme commander made the danger somehow all the more compelling. A nation that had come to live with, and in some erudite military and scientific circles even love the Bomb as a deterrent, now felt horribly vulnerable.

Suddenly the world's only superpower had to confront the threat of "loose nukes," "dirty bombs," and other offspring of the proliferation of nuclear weapons to those not advanced in the high art of their civilized management.

During the Cold War, concerns over the nuclear threat were assuaged by the conviction that the superpower leaders in charge of the more than 25,000 nuclear weapons would be constrained by the mutual assured destruction (MAD, appropriately, was the official policy acronym), were the bombs they so assiduously stockpiled ever to be used in a first-strike and retaliatory response.

Suddenly, after 9/11, we were faced with the prospect, stoked by the alarms of our leaders, of those weapons in the hands of men so deranged as to welcome their own death. That probably wouldn't include Saddam Hussein or any other head of state not given to sacrificing this world's pleasures for those of another, for they would be well aware that retaliation from nations with much bigger arsenals would swiftly eliminate them and everything else they held dear. But might they not surreptitiously pass those, and other so-called weapons of mass destruction, on to stateless terrorists more inclined to suicide?

Though theoretically possible, it is far less likely that the religiously inclined terrorist would have obtained weaponry of any sort from the secular Saddam, who ruthlessly killed any members of al Qaeda found on his turf. A place like Pakistan, where A. Q. Khan, the Father of the Islamic Bomb, was freely proliferating nuke material to North Korean communists and Iranian Islamists alike, would be far more promising. As opposed to Iraq, which didn't have a functioning WMD program, Pakistan already had built dozens of nuclear bombs.

Not willing to let the facts get in the way of their good story line, the Bush administration ignored Pakistan's nuclear transgressions and previous close ties to the Taliban sponsors of bin Laden and even lifted the sanctions that had been imposed by Bill Clinton in retaliation for Pakistan's nuclear test. Instead, the Bush administration's narrative of nukes passing from rogue nation to al Qaeda terrorists centered on Iraq, a nation that had neither of those critical props but did possess other useful attributes.

One was oil. Less than three months before the invasion, Thomas Friedman, the *New York Times* columnist who supported overthrowing Saddam, was candid enough to admit in a January 5, 2003, column entitled "A War for Oil?" that "Any war we launch in Iraq will certainly be—in part—about oil. To deny that is laughable." He then went on to refute the WMD excuse:

> I say this possible Iraq war is partly about oil because it is impossible to explain the Bush team's behavior otherwise. Why are they going after Saddam Hussein with the 82nd Airborne and North Korea with diplomatic kid gloves—when North Korea already has nuclear weapons, the missiles to deliver them, a record of selling dangerous weapons to anyone with cash, 100,000 U.S. troops in its missile range and a leader who is even more

cruel to his own people than Saddam? One reason, of course, is that it is easier to go after Saddam. But the other reason is oil—even if the president doesn't want to admit it.

So it came to pass that the subject of nuclear bombs and the means to deliver them was transformed from what was once a seriously considered and central concern of U.S. national security policy to a giddy propaganda sideshow of alarmist sound bites. The warning by Condoleezza Rice about a "mushroom cloud," and the president's citation of phony enriched uranium sales from Niger to Iraq were all intended not to confront the serious problem of nuclear proliferation to terrorists and rogue nations but to justify invading a country that had completely ended its WMD programs.

Nor did this playing loose with the specter of WMD by an administration that used the prospect of nuclear annihilation as a political ploy evoke all that much concern among foreign policy pundits. Some hawks, like neolib Kenneth Pollack and his neocon counterpart Richard Perle, continued to insist past the point of reason, months after the invasion, that the nonexistent weapons would be found. Others actually blamed Saddam Hussein for tricking us. However, the most alarmingly cynical response came from those who said that getting it right about WMD didn't really matter that much.

Or at all, in the view of Thomas Friedman, who again tried to justify the war in his *New York Times* article, "Because We Could," on June 4, 2003, three months after the invasion: "The failure of the Bush team to produce any weapons of mass destruction (WMD's) in Iraq is becoming a big, big story. But is it the real story we should be concerned with? No. It was the wrong issue before the war, and it's the wrong issue now."

Friedman wrote:

> The "real reason" for this war, which was never
> stated, was that after 9/11 America needed to hit
> someone in the Arab-Muslim world. Afghanistan
> wasn't enough. Because a terrorism bubble had
> built up over there—a bubble that posed a real
> threat to the open societies of the West needed to
> be punctured. . . . The only way to puncture that
> bubble was for American soldiers, men and women,
> to go into the heart of the Arab-Muslim world,
> house to house, and make clear that we are ready
> to kill, and to die, to prevent our open society from
> being undermined by this terrorism bubble. Smash-
> ing Saudi Arabia or Syria would have been fine. But
> we hit Saddam for one simple reason: because we
> could, and because he deserved it and because he
> was right in the heart of that world.

That you have the right to send troops house to house hitting
people in a country that had nothing to do with 9/11 "because
we could" is the classic statement of an imperial bully. But we
Americans are never imperialists because we always have freedom
on our mind. Why didn't Bush just tell us, instead of all this nonsense about nukes and al Qaeda, that creating an open society in
Iraq is all we cared about? That's Friedman's complaint:

> But because the Bush team never dared to spell
> out the real reason for the war, and (wrongly) felt
> that it could never win public or world support for
> the right reasons and the moral reasons, it opted
> for the "stated reason": the notion that Saddam

had weapons of mass destruction that posed an immediate threat to America. I argued before the war that Saddam posed no such threat to America, and had no links with al Qaeda, and that we couldn't take the nation to war "on the wings of a lie." I argued that Mr. Bush should fight this war for the right reasons and the moral reasons. But he stuck with this W.M.D. argument for P.R. reasons.

But playing with the threat of nuclear proliferation for "P.R. reasons" is as dangerous a rhetorical ploy as one can imagine. That is particularly true coming from the president of a nation that invented and used these heinous devices to kill hundreds of thousands of people, and which continues to maintain and "improve" the world's largest stockpile of these civilization-ending weapons.

Nukes do matter; they threaten the very existence of life on this planet, and appropriating that all-important concern as mere cover for other agendas does humanity itself a major, if not ultimately fatal, disservice. Nuclear weapons are still the only weapons truly deserving of the label "weapons of mass destruction," and lumping those civilization zappers in with chemical and biological weapons, though obviously frightening in their own right, masks the fundamentally different order of danger that nuclear weapons represent.

Consider the consequences if that had been even a primitive low-kiloton bomb, say of the Hiroshima variety, that took down the World Trade Center. It would have also obliterated the financial, intellectual, and media center of the United States. Given the attacks on civil liberties and other irrationalities that followed 9/11, a nuclear attack resulting in hundreds of thousands of dead and wounded would most likely have led to the water-boarding of America's experiment in representative democracy.

Trivializing the issue of nuclear proliferation, and raising false alarms about nonexistent threats while ignoring real ones, demonstrates a reckless disregard for our very survival. Some will dismiss that idea as sophomoric in tone, or woefully outdated with the end of the Cold War, but it is a sentiment that George W. Bush once embraced just as fervently. That was in a speech he gave as a presidential candidate on May 23, 2000, expressing a consensus view of what was then still the Republican Party foreign policy establishment, as demonstrated by the Ronald Reagan and Bush I alumni gathered around him for the then Texas governor's first major foreign policy speech. With the possible exception of Rumsfeld, there wasn't a recognizable neocon among them.

> Today, I am here with some of our nation's leading [Republican] statesmen and defense experts [former Secretaries of State Henry Kissinger and George Shultz, former Defense Secretary Donald Rumsfeld, former National Security Adviser Brent Scowcroft, and former chair of the Joint Chiefs of Staff Colin Powell]. And there is broad agreement that our nation needs a new approach to nuclear security that matches a new era.
>
> When it comes to nuclear weapons, the world has changed faster than U.S. policy. The emerging security threats to the United States, its friends and allies, and even to Russia, now come from rogue states, terrorist groups and other adversaries seeking weapons of mass destruction and the means to deliver them. Threats also come from insecure

nuclear stockpiles and the proliferation of dangerous technologies. Russia itself is no longer our enemy. The Cold War logic that led to the creation of massive stockpiles on both sides is now outdated. . . .

We should not keep weapons that our military planners do not need. These unneeded weapons are the expensive relics of dead conflicts. And they do nothing to make us more secure. In addition, the United States should remove as many weapons as possible from high-alert, hair-trigger status—another unnecessary vestige of Cold War confrontation. Preparation for quick launch—within minutes after warning of an attack—was the rule during the era of superpower rivalry. But today, for two nations at peace, keeping so many weapons on high alert may create unacceptable risks of accidental or unauthorized launch.

Bush's commitment to steep cuts in the nuclear arsenals of both nations and stepped-up efforts to prevent proliferation was clear, and he was right to blast the Democrats for failing to move on this: "The Clinton-Gore administration has had over seven years to bring the U.S. force posture into the post–Cold War world. Instead, they remained locked in a Cold War mentality. It is time to leave the Cold War behind, and defend against the new threats to the 21st Century."

Toward that end, Bush promised to "build effective missile defense, based on the best available options, at the earliest possible date." But in the spirit of Ronald Reagan in his meetings with Gorbachev, Bush emphasized that missile defense, when combined with steep cuts in nuclear weapons, was good for both nations: "there are positive, practical ways to demonstrate to Russia that we are no longer enemies. Russia, our allies and the world need to understand our intentions. America's development of missile defenses is a search for security, not a search for advantage. America should rethink the requirements for nuclear deterrence in a new security environment."

Bush's view on the subject, as reflected by the who's who of experts present, was consistent with the nuclear arms control position that had developed in Reagan's last years after he embraced Gorbachev and that was continued into the administration of Bush I. It is a view that weds missile defense to arms control in a package that attempts to appeal to then Soviet and now Russian fears that missile defense is aimed at giving the United States a shield behind which it could launch an attack on their nation.

Before 9/11, when Bush met with Putin in that famous summit embrace on June 16, 2001, the U.S. president was asked if Putin was "a man that Americans can trust." He replied, "I will answer the question. I looked the man in the eye. I found him to be very straightforward and trustworthy. We have a very good dialogue. I was able to get a sense of his soul; a man deeply committed to his country and the best interests of his country. And I appreciated so very much the frank dialogue."

That frank dialogue involved agreement, as Bush said, on establishing "a new relationship beyond that of the old Cold War mentality" and disagreement on missile defense and the restrictions imposed on it by the 1972 ABM treaty. The overall mood was as upbeat as it gets, and the stated assumption of both leaders was that their common commitment to a unified front against terrorism and other world problems would lead to an ever-closer connection. The opposite happened over the next five years.

The Russians opposed the U.S. invasion of Iraq and attempted to block confrontation with Iran. Gone was the rosy expectation of a common front in combating the terrorism that had afflicted both nations, often from the same source. What drove Bush and Putin far apart was, more than anything else, the nuclear issue, as Bush's rosy projections of ending the Cold War nuclear standoff gave way to increased U.S. spending on nuclear weapons as well as missile defense. The contradictions of such a policy were summarized by Lawrence Korb, who had served as Assistant Secretary of Defense in the Reagan administration, who pointed out in an October 25, 2007, commentary in the *Asheville Citizen-Times* that "We spend about $17 billion [a year] to maintain and modernize an arsenal of 10,000 nuclear weapons, each with twenty times the destructive power of Hiroshima."

Oddly, in the midst of its much-ballyhooed war on terror, the Bush administration found an opportunity to justify building new nuclear weapons, which Korb questioned: "How can we use these warheads against al Qaeda cells buried within civilian populations around the world? How many warheads does it take to deter other nuclear powers, such as Russia and China or potential nuclear powers like North Korea or Iran?"

Korb also excoriated the increased spending on missile defense:

> Since its conception as "Star Wars" in the 1980s, missile defense has persisted in our military budgets and political debates without the Soviet menace and without ever proving its operational effectiveness.
>
> How much money is missile defense worth to defeat a low-order threat? It would be easy to dismiss missile defense as a partisan chess piece if it

weren't so costly. We have spent $160 billion over the twenty-four-year lifespan of missile defense and plan to sink approximately $8 billion more next year. And these dollar-figures don't include the diplomatic costs—both to our allies and our arms control agreements with Russia—of insisting on deploying a dysfunctional weapons system that is still unproven.

As the first journalist to whom Reagan confided his enthusiasm for developing a missile defense system, back when I interviewed him in 1980 at some length for the *Los Angeles Times*, it seems bizarre that this idea has persisted beyond the collapse of the Soviet Union. Reagan proposed building such a system as an alternative to the MAD, or mutual assured destruction policy, that viewed the threat of survivable massive retaliation by the United States after a Soviet first strike as the only effective means of containing the nuclear threat. Reagan wanted something more than that dismal prospect of killing many of them after they have destroyed almost all of us, and he became convinced that the science was at hand to accomplish that.

The basis of that optimism, relayed to Reagan by Livermore's Edward Teller, the Father of the Hydrogen Bomb, was something called the nuclear-pumped X-ray laser. It was a futuristic weapon that totally failed to deliver on its earlier promise and has been abandoned. Had it worked—had it proved possible to harness the power of a nuclear explosion in space to produce a huge number of lethal rays to destroy missiles in flight—then the plausibility of missile defense could be argued. The science failed, the early optimism was based on totally false test results, and the program since has moved in less dramatic technological directions.

Whatever the value of missile defense as a tool in the great power standoff of the Cold War, it is difficult to justify continuing the program in the post–Cold War world. Clearly, any such enemy missile would be targeted and eliminated before it was deployed, let alone launched. Why would the United States, rather than taking the weapon out on the ground, wait to respond to the threat only during that short period after launch, when interception would be much more difficult? A rogue nation's attempt to deploy the weapon would be observed easily and thwarted with conventional weapons. However the hawks try to spin it, there is simply no real application of this weapon in the new post–Cold War world.

But the Cold War was threatening to return over this issue. By the last years of the Bush II presidency, relations with Russia were strained, arms control treaties had been torn up, and weapons and troops redeployed in what was interpreted by some as signs of a new Cold War. Bush junked the Anti-Ballistic Missile Treaty and went ahead with plans to install antimissile stations in Poland and the Czech Republic to which the Russians objected.

On November 30, 2007, Putin, three days before his party's sweeping electoral victory in the Russian parliament, signed a law suspending Russia's participation in the Conventional Armed Forces in Europe (CFE) treaty agreed upon two decades earlier. The agreement limited the number of weapons and troops that NATO and the old Soviet Union could deploy in Western Europe and the western portion of Russia.

The move, a response to the antimissile deployment, had been suggested six months previously by Putin during a lengthy press conference. Asked by a reporter for the *Wall Street Journal* what he would do in the face of Bush's decision, Putin cited the CFE and noted:

We have not just stated that we are ready to comply with the treaty, like certain others have done. We really are implementing it: we have removed all of our heavy weapons from the European part of Russia and put them behind the Urals. We have reduced our Armed Forces by 300,000. We have taken several other steps required by the [CFE]. But what have we seen in response? Eastern Europe is receiving new weapons, two new military bases are being set up in Romania and in Bulgaria, and there are two new missile launch areas—a radar in Czech Republic and missile systems in Poland. And we are asking ourselves the question: what is going on? Russia is disarming unilaterally. But if we disarm unilaterally then we would like to see our partners be willing to do the same thing in Europe. On the contrary, Europe is being pumped full of new weapons systems. And of course we cannot help but be concerned.

The antimissile system was defended by Bush as necessary in order to defend against missiles from North Korea and Iran. Putin pointed out that Iran didn't have ICBMs and that North Korea was too far removed from those stations for their placement to make sense. Then, in response to a question about the apparent deterioration in his once close personal relationship with Bush, Putin stated:

I would not want you to suffer from the illusion that we have fallen out of love with anyone. But I sometimes think to myself: why are they doing all this? Why are our American partners trying so obstinately to deploy a missile defense system in Europe when—and this is perfectly obvious—it is not needed to defend against Iranian—or even more obvious—North Korean missiles. . . . Is it perhaps to ensure that we carry out these retaliatory measures? And to prevent a further rapprochement between Russia and Europe?

It is an important question, even though the mass media in the United States ignored it along with the rest of Putin's remarks. Why, indeed, given that an antiballistic missile system so situated could be used to give the United States an advantage in the balance of terror that still existed between the two nations with their thousands of nuclear weapons on hair-trigger alert?

Why does missile defense persist as a major goal of Republican politicians, and why has Bush allowed it to derail his earlier plans to build a close relationship with the Russians? After all, we are talking here about shooting down intercontinental ballistic missiles with technology that is difficult and expensive if not impossible to develop. These are not weapons designed to take out Scud missiles. If Iran were to develop an ICBM and arm it with a nuclear bomb, it would not be all that difficult to eliminate before it was deployed in a threatening manner using conventional U.S. forces.

I do not have the answer, but it is possible that Bush genuinely believes, despite evidence to the contrary, that anti-ICBM defense eventually will be made to work and thereby make us safer. That he could believe this is no more surprising than a belief in other weapons systems marketed by military contractors and pushed by their hawkish lobbyists and political friends.

There has been a lot of profit made off missile defense by the major military contractors, and they lobby long and hard for new funding. For the ideological hawks, the missile system also has the value, cited by Putin, of disrupting closer relations between Russia and its former adversaries. If that is their goal, they have been immensely successful.

Near the end of his eight years in office, the pre-9/11 Bush had been transformed fully from an advocate of a post–Cold War foreign policy that stressed mutual cooperation, even with old adversaries, into a bellicose advocate of the American Century. In response to a question from the German magazine *Der Spiegel* about "the deterioration of your relations with America," Putin alluded to his once very close relationship with Bush that had obviously soured:

> One can hardly use the same terminology in international relations, in relations between countries, that would apply to relationships between people—especially during their honeymoon or as they prepare to go to the Civil Registry Office.
>
> Throughout history, interests have always been the main organizing principle for relations between states and on the international arena. And the more civilized these relations become, the clearer it is that one's own interests must be balanced against the interest of other countries. And one must be able to find compromises to resolve the most difficult problems and issues.
>
> One of the major difficulties today is that certain members of the international community are absolutely convinced that their opinion is the correct one.

What was at issue in the battle over Bush's nuclear policy was the inherent tension between the world vision of his father and Reagan in his last years, and that of the neocon hawks and their allies in the military-industrial complex who were deeply wary of the first President Bush's "new world order," in which trade and diplomacy were emphasized over the military-based unilateralism advocated by the neocons in their Project for the New American Century.

In the process, the arms control treaties of the Cold War came under fire as the Bush administration increasingly embraced the notion that nuclear weapons might be usable, even against opponents who did not possess them. While it is true that the United States has never disavowed the first use of nuclear weapons, and indeed is the only nation that has in fact used them, it had been assumed with the end of the Cold War that the arsenals, as well as the number of weapons deployed in hair-trigger launch mode, would be much reduced.

Unfortunately, during the eight years of the Clinton administration, little progress was made in that direction, as George W. Bush pointed out during the 2000 campaign. In his first years in office, Bush attempted to redress that, and he and Putin signed off on what is known as the Moscow Agreement to reduce weapons on launch to several thousand by the year 2012. But that is still a massive quantity of explosive power left on hair-trigger alert, meaning a president would have to decide within twelve minutes whether to launch—and thereby to destroy most of the life on Earth.

However, one need not launch nuclear weapons for them to be extremely dangerous. The risk of those weapons getting loose from the command structure, for example, was underscored in the "Bent Spear" incident that came to light in August of 2007. A B-52 bomber presumably ferrying decommissioned cruise missiles was accidently loaded with six that were nuclear armed and ferried about the country with their location and potent nature unknown for a full day and a half. Four commanders were relieved of their duty and sixty-five airmen decertified from handling nuclear weapons over that unnerving episode. Human error takes on a whole different meaning when tens of thousands of nuclear weapons are concerned.

But the problem is not just with the accidental threat. As part of a new strategy called "tailored deterrence," the Bush administration produced more usable nuclear weapons to add to America's post–Cold War stockpile. As an October 29, 2007, Congressional Research Service report put it, "Tailored deterrence differs from Cold War deterrence in that it explicitly notes that U.S. nuclear weapons could be used in attacks against a number of nations that might have developed and deployed chemical and biological weapons, even if they did not possess nuclear weapons." The CRS report observed pointedly that "There has been little discussion of this concept, either in Congress or in the public at large." Critics of this policy, the CRS notes, claim it shows a "growing willingness of the United States to resort to nuclear weapons use before other means—including diplomacy and conventional force—have been employed and exhausted."

The problem is that if the United States finds nuclear weapons usable, why should other nations refrain from developing some of their own? For the one nation that killed hundreds of thousands of Japanese civilians with nuclear weapons, and which has long refused to pledge not to use them again in a preemptive strike, to now develop new nuclear devices, including bunker busters, puts us on the side of those who believe nukes are just another weapon and belong in a civilized nation's arsenal. It's an awful message to be sending out to a troubled and deeply divided world.

Long after he had served as secretary of defense, Robert McNamara, along with former National Security Adviser McGeorge Bundy and others, called for the abolishment of nuclear weapons. They were attempting to kick-start a debate that the country has never really had, but they failed. There is a black hole in the American political imagination concerning the fact that we are the only nation to have ever used the ultimate weapon. We have never faced up to our responsibility for having committed what may be the ultimate terrorist act, taking the lives of hundreds of thousands of totally innocent fishermen and the like who had not voted their emperor into office, nor were they in any way consulted about their nation's decision to launch war against the United States. They were simply used as props in our effort to demonstrate the power of the bomb.

Since that time, except for that New York minute when Reagan and Gorbachev considered the zero-nuclear-weapons option, American politicians have avoided it as a third rail issue. It has become unthinkable to consider doing away with the unthinkable weapon.

Chapter 10

BUDGET BLUES

In the fall of 2007, six years into the war on terror, President George W. Bush sent a budget to Congress that made it clear that the bad guys had won. All of them, from the murderous Osama bin Laden, spectacularly branded the new villain of international terrorism and now gleefully baiting us into bankruptcy with shoddy videotapes; to the merely mendacious American politicians who gained power by exploiting those newfound terror fears; and on to the predictable war profiteers who finally had a compelling, if never precisely defined, enemy to justify Cold War business as usual despite the bothersome dissolution of the Soviet Union.

Actually, the profit situation was even more promising than during the Cold War, which had been deprived of its once shrill sense of urgency by Richard Nixon's pursuit of détente with the Soviets, eventually leading to mutual caps on arms developments. Yes, things had looked up again in the 1980s, when Ronald Reagan revived the old rhetoric. And while his actual commitment of troops into battle was far lower than that of any other postwar president, his get-tough language—and much more important, the spending spree it incited—brought solace to the defense industry and its acolytes in the Pentagon and related think tanks. But then came Reagan's late-term affair with Mikhail Gorbachev. Although their union did not lead to the abolishment of all nuclear weapons as the peace-smitten couple had hoped when they embarked on their Reykjavik, Iceland, honeymoon in 1986, new arms caps were imposed. Five years later, the Cold War came to an end, thanks mostly to Gorbachev, who unexpectedly deprived us of an enemy.

That fact was acknowledged during Bush I's administration, when even hawks like his defense secretary, Dick Cheney, were pushing serious cuts in the military budget. Bill Clinton, being a Democrat and therefore susceptible to the "soft on defense" charge, lamely tried to throw more money at the military than Bush had, but the case to be made for such spending was getting ludicrous. Even the wars that Clinton dragged us into in the Balkans and Africa, which Bush I had resisted, did not involve an enemy that required an increase in the already vastly excessive U.S. military arsenal. In short, military spending was going nowhere fast after bottoming at a Defense Department 2000 budget of $354.4 billion; quite a drop, in constant 2007 dollars, from Reagan's high of $517.8 billion in 1985.

The second President Bush had made some noises as a candidate that he would strengthen America's military defenses, but in his first eight months in office he did little of the sort. Meanwhile, Donald Rumsfeld, his secretary of defense, was frightening the heck out of the military-industrial guys by going on about a leaner and meaner military budget for the modern age.

Panic was in the air—until the World Trade Center towers went down. There is little doubt that were it not for 9/11, Bush administration members would never have dared to push for major military spending increases. And if they had been stupid enough to risk losing public support by wasting the peace dividend to pacify defense industry supporters, Congress would not have gone along. But 9/11 did happen, and by 2008, the military budget was raised hundreds of billions, exceeding the highest level of Cold War spending.

That last sentence slides off the brain. The military budget is impossible to comprehend, let alone explain to others in a way that will make them care. Okay, so it's not *literally* impossible—most of the relevant numbers can be aggregated, parsed, and analyzed by professionals—but by the time the pros get through the numbers, most folks will have tuned out.

Not so the army of lobbyists fighting to grab every loose buck, the politicians concerned about contributions and constituents' jobs, and the military brass who find reflections of their careers and egos in new weapons systems. But ordinary taxpayers have a hard enough time imagining the difference between a million and a billion, let alone holding those who spend trillions accountable. Several trillion is what Nobel Prize–winning economist Joseph Stiglitz and Harvard budget expert Linda Bilmes estimated the war in Iraq had cost by 2007, after adding in the long-term costs of injury care, interest payments on the debt incurred, and the like.

But as I write this chapter, a news story appears on my computer, and suddenly I have a measurement for the opportunity cost of the war. President George W. Bush vetoed additional funding of $7 billion a year for an expansion of the federal children's health insurance plan, as he found it too costly—Bush had wanted to allocate $1 billion more to the program. It is instructive to consider that the president was holding the line on a spending difference of just $6 billion only two weeks after he had asked Congress to appropriate yet another $50 billion in "supplementary" funding, mostly for the Iraq war. That amount was on top of the $147 billion in supplementary funds already requested for the budget year 2008.

The term "supplementary" refers to funding above and beyond the $506.9 billion in regular budget requests for the Defense Department for that year. What you get or don't get for all of that money is discussed throughout this book, but let's focus here on only the additional $7 billion amount that the president refused to give Congress for a children's health-care program that had broad bipartisan congressional support as well as that of many governors and mayors across the country. Incidentally, the bill passed by Congress proposed covering part of that additional expense with an increase in the cigarette tax, but even so, the president vetoed it in the name of fiscal responsibility.

As Senator Edward M. Kennedy, one of the authors of the child health bill, observed following Bush's expending only the fourth veto of his more than six years in office, "Today we learned that the same president who is willing to throw away a half trillion dollars in Iraq is unwilling to spend a small fraction of that amount to bring health care to American children." As I read that remark by the liberal Massachusetts senator, I knew that his point would be lost in the media world, and it was. In the coverage of the president's veto of the bill, it was rare for there to be even the slightest reference to what economists call the "opportunity cost," a comparison, as Kennedy had made, between the benefit to American taxpayers of money spent on defense as opposed to social programs.

Consider the different degree of scrutiny involved here. The amount in question, $7 billion, would represent about a couple of weeks' cost of the Iraq war, which by this point a majority of Americans saw no point in continuing. Yet the president's supplementary budget request of an amount thirty times greater for Iraq went largely unquestioned, even by congressional and media critics of the war. The much smaller expenditure extending health care to an additional 3.4 million uninsured American children was ever so closely examined before being blocked by the president's veto.

One can easily find many examples of $7 billion a year wasted on weapons systems that the military services don't even want but which, because they are heavily lobbied for, get easily folded into the overall Defense Department budget. An example cited previously was Senator Lieberman's Virginia-class submarine, built in his home state of Connecticut. He has pushed for funding for two subs a year at a combined cost of over $5 billion.

The notion that this was a wasteful entitlement was rarely suggested. Yet big-ticket defense commitments represent entitlements in much the same way as a child health-care program does. Once a weapon system is begun, its continued financing will be taken for granted by those who benefit from its production. They will lobby for funding in the future, and the weapon will continue to be produced long after it has any useful military function.

President Bush signed off on a budget including many such programs that the defense contractors assuredly feel will be entitled to renewal year after year, but he doesn't refer to those expenditures as entitlements. That is a word he, and most conservative politicians, reserve as a rhetorical weapon for criticizing social programs, like children's health care, that they prefer to regard as costly in the long run and not truly necessary.

The basic argument is as simple as it is fundamentally erroneous. The assumption is that funding for social programs should be viewed as entitlements because they become permanent, whereas the national security side of the ledger represents a necessary response to a state of emergency, the implication being that the obligation will decline or disappear altogether when the emergency is over or the war has been won. But that does not accurately describe the economy of the United States, which ever since World War II has lived with a permanently colossal military budget irrespective of the degree of perceived danger in the larger world. Now, with a permanent war on terror, it is even safer to state that the excuse for the military budget will not decline in intensity, and therefore neither will the expenditures.

Quite the opposite; while most of the social problems, including poor schools, inadequate housing, and impoverished children, can be kept out of the sight lines of the more prosperous who set the political agenda, a foreign policy crisis can easily be stoked in response to any sagging interest in defense allocations. Such demands, even when they are used to justify weapons that have nothing to do with the perceived threat, will always carry with them urgency not felt for uninsured kids studying in inadequate schools—or just about any other obligation of the government to improve the well-being of its citizenry.

Just look at a pie chart of all federal spending for discretionary funds, meaning money not already committed by law to Social Security, Medicare and Medicaid, and other obligations fixed by law, such as servicing the national debt. A good chunk of the latter sum derives from past military spending. The money that is available for what is called discretionary spending is the accurate one to use in assessing the options open to Congress and the president as they annually assess competing needs in the society.

A pie chart prepared by the National Priorities Project tells that story, and it is one on which apologists for the military-industrial complex don't want you to focus, but it is the relevant one in considering the choices as to how we spend our tax dollars on federal programs. The discretionary budget encompasses the full range of that federal spending, from programs to protect natural resources and the environment (3 percent) to veterans' benefits and services (4 percent). Transportation garners a scant 2 percent, and the very important category that includes education, training, employment, and social services gets another 6 percent. Care about science, space, and other technology programs? That's another 3 percent; health programs get 5 percent. Those are all very important programs concerning scientific research, the education of children, and the care of veterans. But all of the money not devoted to the current military obligations of the proposed 2008 budget, all of it, added up to 41 percent.

Compared to that figure, the national defense piece of the pie came in at a whopping 59 percent. That means that just about six out of every ten dollars available to the federal government to meet the myriad needs of the American people went to the military-industrial complex. Oddly, despite the massive part of the pie devoted to the military, it is subject to far less public scrutiny than even small pieces of what remains for the rest.

Pretty shocking given the imbalance in attention, but as was illustrated by the mad dash to throw money at the defense industry after 9/11 for programs that had nothing to do with that event, when a national security crisis is in the offing all bets are off as to budgetary constraint. The shirking of concerned scrutiny by so-called fiscal conservatives is the norm, and while indulging vast excess in this quarter, they salvage their conscience or at least their claim on the conservative brand name by aiming wrathful deliberation at already underfunded domestic programs.

The problem is that this high level of defense spending places an enormous burden on all of the other non-military programs that are left competing for the 41 percent of discretionary federal dollars not soaked up by defense. This competition for domestic-program funding will extend well into the future as the retiring baby boomers drive up the cost of huge entitlement programs—Social Security and Medicare, for example. That is because the madcap military spending of the Bush years wiped out the budget surplus of the Clinton era, and instead of contributing to a decline in the national debt, the Bush years have seen it spiral upward.

As a result, the debt will have to be paid off by future generations. Those interest payments, in the tens of billions of dollars, represent money that will not be available to do all of the things that American taxpayers want their tax money used for, from hurricane relief to health research. The fact that those interest payments are increasingly paid to foreign holders of our debt in China, Japan, and elsewhere means that debt servicing does not even efficiently pump money back into the domestic economy.

That is an important consideration when encountering yet another common apology for spiraling defense costs. Yes, the military hawks concede, current defense expenditures have increased our national debt, but it is money we owe to ourselves. Therefore it is not really a drain on future generations, who will be receiving interest on the government paper they hold, and that will represent more money available for domestic consumer spending. This is an increasingly specious argument when one considers the steep rise in the percentage of the U.S. debt owed not to U.S. citizens but to foreigners.

The point here is that money spent on the military is not free money, as the defense lobbyists and their political allies imply. Those programs may be necessary, but we should recognize that the cost is dear for both current and future generations—a matter of common sense so obvious that this time around, the neoconservatives at first attempted to hide the enormous cost of their projected war in Iraq by suggesting, as Paul Wolfowitz did so famously and falsely, that Iraqi oil revenues would pay for it. But he was hardly alone.

This is not a new propaganda ploy for the proponents of empire, for it is always claimed by apologists for imperial adventure that the foreign spoils will not only easily finance the cost of the expedition but reap profits far beyond. The reality is that empires are not cost effective; the price of policing a hostile population while you make off with their treasures always exceeds the cost of the occupation, and in the end it is the economy of the mother country that is bankrupted in the process.

Of course the true cost of empire is never considered when the foreign adventures are first undertaken, and no matter whether the stated cause is patriotism, God, profit, or, as is most often the case, an unseemly combo of the above, there is never time to consult the party-pooper accountants to ask what this binge might end up costing us. There is an infectious giddiness that inevitably accompanies the rush to war, and any sense of fiscal caution is dismissed as inappropriate at a moment when the nation's honor as well as survival is on the line. Those are not times to quibble about cost, and the warmongers and other empire builders know well how to sing that sultry song.

It remains for others to pick through the pieces afterward and provide a reckoning, but unfortunately the bad news only registers in the hangover stage when the public and the politicians who deceived them just want to forget about it all. That explains the tepid reception to the study on the cost of the war conducted by Joseph Stiglitz and Linda Bilmes that estimated the war in Iraq had incurred, by February 2008, long-term costs of $3 trillion, and that does not include interest on the debt in-curred. Despite being printed in the still popular *Rolling Stone* magazine and referenced throughout the Internet, their study did not generate much debate as to whether the continued oc-cupation of Iraq was cost effective in the slightest.

What Nobel Prize–winner Stiglitz and his Harvard col-league dealt with, and most politicians and media pundits tended to ignore, was the ultimate cost of the war after the fighting stops. For example, the cost of dealing with seriously wounded U.S. military personnel most often will continue through their lifetime, as does ministering to the needs of all veterans from the war, a significant number of whom will have long-term readjustment problems. Stiglitz and Bilmes estimated that the losses from veterans who had suffered injury alone would run to $35 billion.

Not only were the long-term fiscal consequences of the war rarely taken into account, but even the current costs, those fig-ures in the annual budget and supplementary allocations, were bought on the government's credit card. By refusing to raise taxes, Bush spared the public the immediate cost of the war and billed it to future generations.

The absence of a pay-as-you-go approach to the war was, like the use of a volunteer army and contractor mercenaries as opposed to drafted conscripts, intended to undermine opposi-tion to the war. It was a ploy as effective as it was cynical, and public opposition to the war, although it became the majority view in polls, never crystallized as urgent pressure on Congress or the president because the pain of the war in the short run was mitigated.

But the cost of the war has been staggering, not only due to the huge amount soaked up by military actions in Iraq and Afghanistan, but because 9/11 released the floodgates on the entire military program. National defense outlays were higher in 2008 than at any time since the end of World War II, even after discounting the impact of inflation. That means we were annually spending more in constant dollars than in the long Cold War dispute with the Russian Soviets and Chinese communists, despite their massive armies.

The enemies defined by the 9/11 attacks possess no army, and yet the military budget for conventional weapons and forces has ballooned. In a revealing pie chart prepared by the National Priorities Project, conventional military spending shows up as 89 percent of the total of military spending, whereas spending for homeland security is a scant 7 percent, and for preventive measures only 4 percent. This last item covers securing nuclear materials throughout the world, as well as U.S. participation in multilateral peacekeeping and diplomatic efforts.

As the report of the National Priorities Project, an independent and credible watchdog, analyzing the budget for 2005 concluded, "almost nine dollars was spent on the military for every dollar spent on all other non-military security tools combined." Those numbers reflect an obsessive focus on the Cold War–era military threat, much of which dissipated with the collapse of Soviet communism and the preoccupation of the Chinese communists with turning their economy into a marketing rather than military powerhouse.

While the threat of terrorism is real enough, the military budget profoundly ignores the shifting battleground. The result is that the 9/11 attacks became an occasion for firing up a massive military without a substantial military state opponent in sight. At the same time, there was no comparable outburst of energy and programs reflected in the budget to meet the threat posed by stateless terrorists.

Ironically, there was a dramatic increase in the sale of

U.S.–produced armaments to other nations, including those such as Saudi Arabia and Pakistan, which increased the risks of war. The United States is the world's leading international arms merchant. Liberated Iraq had become part of the lucrative Third World market for arms, and in the fall of 2007 it was announced that the government in Baghdad has signed deals to purchase $1.6 billion in U.S. arms, with another $1.8 billion in contracts slated for early approval.

But other nations including China are also expanding such sales, and in one of the oddest consequences of the Iraq invasion, a very lucrative arms market developed in "liberated" Iraq, with other nations eagerly participating. In October 2007, Iraqi President Jalal Talabani announced that his nation had ordered $100 million of light military equipment from China to equip the Iraqi police force.

The Iraqi police force was notorious for being infiltrated by various militant militias that had used it as an armory and was unable to account for 190,000 weapons supplied by the United States. Those arms can easily find their way to insurgents, and we were confronted with the spectacle that an invasion of Iraq aimed ostensibly at eliminating terrorists was in fact arming them.

During World War II and even in the first decades after the start of the Cold War, U.S. presidents of both parties prided themselves on closely watching defense dollar expenditures as part of their obligation to provide a strong defense. The spending spree after 9/11 put those past efforts at fiscal responsibility to shame.

"Ronald Reagan, in his wildest dreams, would find this simply staggering," noted Gordon Adams, who had been the defense budget director under Clinton, speaking of Bush's 2007 budget request for the war. "This is a strategic reach that is almost incomprehensible." Adams, a highly respected defense expert, who under Clinton as White House defense budget director supported spending considerable sums on the military, was not exaggerating.

His outrage was shared by one of the nation's leading defense experts, Lawrence J. Korb, who, responding to the budget requests being presented in October 2007, wrote in a commentary article for the *Iowa City Press-Citizen* September 29, 2007:

> Contrary to the common (and often unquestioned) assumption, spending more money doesn't necessarily buy us more security. The Pentagon currently absorbs more than half of the federal government's discretionary budget—at a whopping $500 billion proposed for next year—surpassing the heights reached in the 1980s when I was President Reagan's assistant secretary of defense. This baseline budget doesn't even include the money spent on the wars in Iraq and Afghanistan. And much like the 1980s, we are spending billions of dollars on weapons systems designed to fight the Soviet superpower. With our resources stretched in the war on terror, it's high time we examined whether the money we spend on defense is actually meeting modern challenges or simply subsidizing outdated thinking.

As examples of the latter, Korb questioned spending $4.5 billion a year to continue production of the F-22 Raptor fighter jet. The jet, 120 of which were already built, had still not been used in combat at the time of Korb's comments, yet clearly they were not needed in any foreseeable situation. "Moreover, the lack of a peer competitor emerging in the skies from another superpower further undermines the supposed 'need' for the F-22. Do we want to invest billions of taxpayer dollars in a plane that busts budgets but adds little to our capabilities?"

Korb did not reference the fact that Lockheed's $300 billion joint strike fighter was already being tested and would make the F-22 redundant.

The defense expenditure explosion under George W. Bush did not represent an extension of the Reagan ideology, as the neocons claimed, but rather a betrayal of it, the reason being that the buildup was unsustainable both politically and financially. A politician as sharp as Reagan would have predicted that the public would grow weary of the government's throwing so much money at a problem without making any progress in addressing it. It's not financially sustainable because the effort to stave off just such public scrutiny had led the Bush administration to pay for it all as a credit card debt held primarily by Chinese, Japanese, and other foreign investors that would give them leverage over U.S. actions in the future.

What irony that one of the main justifications continuously offered by the military hawks for the buildup of the post–Cold War forces is that a Cold War–style enemy, most likely in the form of China, would appear, to make sense of it all. What a contradiction to mortgage the financial future to the same Chinese communist-led government that, according to the neocons who got us into this nightmare, you expect to serve also as your fiercely threatening military adversary.

Chapter 11

THE CHINESE ARE COMING

The enormous capitalist-style success of communist-run China has been the neocon ideologues' worst nightmare. Military confrontation didn't work. The Korean War ended with a stalemate with China, and the United States ignominiously lost its war with the Vietnamese communists, whom U.S. policy had treated as surrogates of Beijing. Nixon's diplomatic opening to China, which the neocons bitterly opposed, ushered in an era of peace, trade, and relative goodwill. There is still hope, among military hawks, that the Chinese enemy will return.

The basis of the neocons' fierce hostility to Nixon's policy of détente, stressing diplomatic overtures to the Soviet and Chinese communist regimes during the Cold War, had been that communism was an immutable enemy bent on world conquest. This fundamentally flawed model of the international threat was accepted as a truism at the onset of the Cold War by a large and bipartisan consensus. Communism was presumed to be internationalist rather than nationalist and incapable of profound change, internally or in its followers' commitment to world revolution. The ironclad hold of the communist ideology was expected to totally dominate their actions in the real world.

It is difficult to grasp now, but this incredibly simplistic and wrongheaded view of the "enemy" was rarely challenged in the decades between the McCarthy scare of the early 1950s and the acknowledgment of the debacle of Vietnam in the late 1960s. During those twenty or so years, despite overwhelming evidence to the contrary, the goal of the communists to proceed with their "timetable for the takeover of the world" was accepted as gospel by most establishment experts in the worlds of media and politics, in their public pronouncements if not their private reservations.

As a result of the mind-numbing hysteria of the witch hunts identified with Senator Joe McCarthy, amplified by wide support—or deafening silence—by the American elite, it became acceptable to embrace a simplistic and hysterical view of the communist threat as the bedrock of U.S. foreign policy, although many in those same rarefied circles knew the idea of an immutable unified communist threat to be absurd. But to dare challenge that patriotic construct was to invite an end to one's career in government, public service, and professional circles. Just why so many people who knew better willingly embraced falsehoods despite breathing the still-free air of America must be left to another inquiry. That intelligent and evidently decent and sincere political leaders in the thousands embraced foreign policy slogans that they knew to be inherently wrong is an unmistakable fact of that era.

Admittedly, it is difficult to understand how anyone with a modicum of knowledge about the rise of communism, first in Russia, then China, and later Vietnam and Cuba, could ever suggest that those movements were driven more by internation-

alist solidarity than nationalist purpose. Yet it is also true that
the Sino-Soviet dispute only came to be accepted in mainstream
American policies after President Richard Nixon and Henry
Kissinger traveled to China to share toasts with the men they
had previously described as the bloodiest international revolutionaries of all. Nixon, who had embraced détente with the
Soviets, then did the same with the Chinese communist leadership explicitly, as he stated frequently, because they represented
nationalist movements deeply at odds with each other, and the
profound differences between them could be exploited by such
diplomatic openings on the part of the United States.

Nixon was right, of course, and it was his diplomacy that
began the unraveling of the Cold War. But while Nixon, who
had risen to prominence as a provincial anticommunist of the
McCarthy school, might have made this discovery only late in
his trajectory toward the presidency, that does not explain the
acquiescence to Cold War mythology on the part of far more
knowledgeable and sophisticated leaders.

The Sino-Soviet split was an obvious reality that began in
earnest back in the late 1920s, when Joseph Stalin clearly indicated his preference for the non-communist leader of China,
Chiang Kai-shek, over the communist upstart Mao Tse-tung.
Stalin was a nationalist and a racist, not a surprising stance for
a bloody tyrant, and his preoccupation was with the "Soviet
Motherland," an unwieldy Slavic coalition that first Lenin
and then Stalin unified through extreme repression. But what
emerged, after the Soviet victory over Germany in the Second
World War, was a Moscow-centric xenophobic entity that
sought not world domination but rather a buffer zone of occupied Eastern European satellite nations.

This, Stalin accomplished until Marshal Tito, head of the
Eastern European communist country Yugoslavia, broke with

the Soviets. Unlike the other satellite-country leaders, Tito owed his power not to the Soviet army but rather to the fight of the partisans he led in World War II. Tito's breakaway from the Soviets in 1948 was at first met with denunciations but eventually was accommodated when it was clear that Yugoslavia would follow a neutral course in the Cold War. But U.S. policy makers and politicians focused on the oppression of the other Eastern European satellites and the acquiescence of their puppet leaders to the Soviets, who as opposed to Tito had no nationalist base. The model of "captive nations" ignored the example of Tito's nationalist independence as well as that of the Chinese communists who rose to power at that time.

Clearly Mao owed very little to the Soviets, having led a revolution based on Chinese peasants and their strengths and concerns. Soviet Premier Nikita Khrushchev's memoirs are only a small part of the evidence that Mao was treated by the Soviet leadership from Stalin on down in a contemptuous and racist manner, and that Mao would have none of it. Mao's China, through all of its ideological twists and turns, never paid heed to the Soviets as leaders of a world movement, and indeed his wildest policies, from the Great Leap Forward to the Cultural Revolution, can be best understood as a reaction to what he thought were the extreme failures of the Soviet bureaucratic model. The Chinese communists under Mao and ever after have been most accurately defined by a fervent nationalism that feeds on the historically grounded suspicions of the intentions of other foreign powers and that certainly at all times has included hostility toward the intentions of the Soviets in greater Russia.

But while actual fighting along the border between the communist Chinese and Soviets preceded the massive commitment of U.S. troops to Vietnam, both Democratic and Republican presidents nonetheless ascribed that war against a Vietnamese national liberation movement that had deep roots in defeating French colonialism to the worldwide battle against something called international communism.

Nixon well understood that this presumption of the unity of communism as a matter of shared ideology was nonsense even as he escalated the Vietnam War, as did presidents Kennedy and Johnson before him. He, like his predecessors, embraced the slogans of a worldwide fight against the scourge of international communism because, as both Johnson and Nixon freely conceded in the tapes they made while in office, it served another agenda: gaining and holding political power. Tragically, Johnson stated quite clearly on those tapes that he could never honestly justify sending a soldier to Vietnam on national security grounds, but that Republican presidential candidate Barry Goldwater would have been able to effectively challenge his patriotism and strength as a leader if he broke with the prevailing myths of the Cold War.

For example, on May 27, 1964, only six months after becoming president, Johnson was recorded on the tapes in a candid conversation with his old Senate buddy, Richard Russell of Georgia, who was then chairman of the all-important Senate Armed Services Committee. That conversation should be burned into the brains of reporters who take politicians' statements on national security at face value:

Johnson: What do you think of this Vietnam thing?
Russell: It's the damn worst mess I ever saw, and I don't like to brag. I never have been right many times in my life. But I knew that we were going to get into this sort of mess when we went in there.
Johnson: That's the way that I've been feeling for six months.

Russell: If I was going to get out, I'd get the same crowd that got rid of old Diem to get rid of these people and get some fellow in there that said he wished to hell we would get out. That would give us a good excuse for getting out. . . .

Johnson: How important is it to us?

Russell: It isn't important a damn bit, with all these new missile systems.

Johnson, later: I've got a little old sergeant that works for me over at the house, and he's got six children, and I just put him up there as the United States Army, Air Force and Navy every time I think about making this decision, and think about sending that father of those six kids in there. And what the hell are we going to get out of his doing it? And it just makes the chills run up my back.

Russell: It does me. I just can't see it.

Later that day there is another tape of Johnson in conversation with his national security adviser, McGeorge Bundy.

Johnson: I don't think it's worth fighting for, and I don't think that we can get out. It just the biggest damn mess I ever saw.

Bundy: It is. It's an awful mess.

Johnson: It's damned easy to get in a war, but it's gonna be awfully hard to extricate yourself if you get in.

For Nixon, the contradiction between truth and political expediency was heightened even more, given that he made his dramatic peace with Red China while escalating the war against Vietnam, a much smaller communist country that was only justified as a target because of its alleged connections with the two communist behemoths of China and the Soviet Union. Surely there was nothing about Vietnam—its resources, military strength, strategic placement, or any other factor other than the symbolism of a small peasant society daring to stand up to the United States and winning—that would justify all of the very costly attention. Yet it was precisely Nixon's peacemaking with China that finally revealed just how absurd was the claim of a threat to the United States from Vietnam.

For the inveterate military hawks, Vietnam had its uses both as a way of stoking the larger menace of communism and as a testing ground to prove the efficacy of modern American weaponry. The problem was, however, that Vietnam failed them on both points; too many Americans came to laugh at the very idea of Vietnam as a threat, and the very expensive weapons, while certainly horribly destructive, causing the death of millions of innocent civilians, had come to give modern militarism a bad name. In the end, by being both immoral and ineffective, the hawks, particularly the emerging neocons, were forced to accept cutting their losses in Vietnam but not compelled to learn the real lesson of that horrible escapade, which is that we were using the people of Vietnam as props in our political theater rather than providing for their well-being. After the unceremonious withdrawal of the United States, there was little sense of any continuing obligation, certainly not reparations for all of the destruction or aid in rebuilding, but even more cynical was the refusal to learn from our series of errors. Just how had we managed to become so preoccupied with the nonexistent threat from Vietnam?

Even more important, what did it say about the much larger specter, the threat of international communism that was the basis of the Cold War? At least with the self-immolation of communism in the Soviet Union, one could argue that the leaders of that country had been forced to face the weakening of the system by an arms race with what could be argued was a more efficient capitalist opponent. I don't subscribe to the view that the Reagan arms buildup forced the Soviets to recognize that they could not keep up and therefore had to go out of business. The reality of nuclear war is that a nation already in possession of thousands of such weapons and the means of inflicting them on its opponents need not build any more for its own survival.

As for poor economic performance relative to the United States raising Soviet citizens' expectations, it should be remembered that dictatorships, no matter their ideological base, have proven quite adept at holding on to power long after they served anyone's but the dictator's needs. The Soviet Union underwent perestroika and glasnost under Gorbachev precisely for the same reason that fundamental change came to China under Deng Xiaoping: The leadership came to realize that focusing on economic growth rather than military power was a more enduring means of their own survival. For the Soviet communists, as opposed to the Chinese, the message came too late, and the change offered was too limited. But in both instances, the lesson they had learned leading to this enormous shift in the ends and the means of governance in their societies was that their power position was best served not by caving in to the demands of their own military establishments but instead by heeding the time-honored injunction to turn swords into plowshares.

As opposed to Gorbachev, the Chinese communist leaders did not give up their power as rulers. Instead, they much enhanced it by changing the entire focus of their nation, revolutionizing its very purpose from that of a militarized statist economy to a state-directed but market-oriented one. They came to stress trade conquest as opposed to military power in protecting the nation and extending its worldwide influence. Given that this change of direction profoundly altered the circumstance of one-fifth of the world's population, it is arguably one of the most important revolutions in the history of the world's people. It is not a revolution that is by any means complete or easy to fully describe as to its origins or to predict its future, but what seems to have been ignored is that it smashes the central myth of the Cold War, which was that communist leaders were incapable of presiding over fundamental reform.

Most observers, without becoming cheerleaders for the Chinese experiment with all its zigzags of accomplishment and failure, would recognize nonetheless that the changes in that country are as profound as those experienced by any other social system, and that they will not be easily reversed. Even most people in Taiwan, the one enduring historic target of Chinese jingoism, be it inspired by communism or nationalism, would concede the former statement. Otherwise, we would not have witnessed the enormous capital investment by Taiwanese businesses on the mainland. Reversals can occur, leaders can say and do irrational and otherwise stupid things, even in boastful democracies with well-educated publics and the restraint of a governmental division of powers and a free media. So maybe China and Taiwan will go to war—dumber things have happened—though the growing trade and travel ties make it less and less probable. At least that's what the Taiwanese investors, who do know the mainland terrain as well as anyone, seem to think.

The evidence points in a far brighter direction: clearly the Chinese leadership, as well as the great mass of people in that country who need to be kept relatively happy, have learned that it is better to make trade than war. What else can they think, after the experience of the first part of this century, when the United States once again got sucked into an old-fashioned imperial disaster in the Third World. Even though the target this time, Iraq as opposed to Vietnam, did contain the enormous potential booty of the world's second largest source of oil, the United States ended up having to pay dearly. While the U.S. wasted more than a trillion dollars on Iraq, including protecting its oil, which drove the price of oil sky-high, the U.S. economy suffered, but the Chinese economy did not.

Although a huge importer of oil, the Chinese went merrily around the world signing contracts to ensure future delivery and simply passed on to consumers in the United States and elsewhere the higher cost of petroleum on top of the price of the finished goods they sold. A Chinese company, as of this writing, was even negotiating for a vast rebuilding contract in Iraq with the U.S.-imposed government. Oil will be shipped to China from the Mideast and elsewhere on shipping lanes protected by U.S. military power because that seems to be what we are now good at, while they do the manufacturing and selling that used to be our specialty.

Hopefully what I have written is correct and the Chinese and the Russians will forswear militarism for trade as the best means of protecting their national interest. It would certainly make for a better world, and it is up to the citizens of those and other countries to make the decisions as to how they are governed and when it is time to do it another way. But that is not the view of the neocons.

They will not give up the ghost of the communist menace as they had imagined it during the Cold War, and for good reason. It is all well and good to go about knocking off broken dictators like Saddam Hussein or even upping the ante in the stupidity sweepstakes and invading Iran. But such an enemy will not an "Evil Empire" make. Rogue regimes just don't cut it for long as fearsome enemies, for they lack the return firepower to justify the enormous cost of an ever-expanding U.S. military machine. As the leaders of France, England, and other failed empires learned, the difficult and costly trick in overthrowing "rogue regimes" is in the occupation: finding appropriate puppets, getting their treasury to pay for the occupation, and setting one regime against the other without having any of the turmoil touch you at home. It never worked very well in the imperial past, but these days it works not at all.

One lesson of Vietnam that should have been learned is that thanks to modern technology, foreign wars are no longer foreign; they are fought on the world population's living room screens, where the costs are difficult to hide. So, too, the blow-back from these adventures, which now come to haunt you at home thanks to international air traffic. As the 9/11 Commission pointed out, the World Trade Center and Pentagon were attacked because Khalid Sheikh Mohammed and Osama bin Laden met each other on a field of battle in Afghanistan, paid for and directed by the United States government. Foreign adventures don't stay foreign for long.

It is true that terrorism, or rather the endless war against terror, provides a fearsome enemy and affords the convenience that an enemy so defined will never be vanquished. There will always be some desperately angry or otherwise deranged humans willing to wreak havoc among us; the problem for the hawks is that such an enemy does not provide a good rationale for a huge and sophisticated military apparatus.

Obviously, in this very different post–Cold War world, neither hundreds of supersonic stealth jet fighters nor sophisticated multibillion-dollar submarines will do anything to stop terrorism at our door. Rather, crack international policing, a larger army of language translators, experts knowledgeable about various religions and cultures, maintaining security at key targets, and getting the CIA and FBI to communicate better are the sorts of efforts that will make us safer. But those tasks do not a military-industrial complex make—for that you need tasks that justify very costly weapons systems.

That is why the neocons so desperately need the Chinese communists. Not the ones who fill the shelves of Costco and Wal-Mart, but the Chicoms of old, the "yellow horde" as once described in racist terms, that threatens us with wile and ingenuity, given to sneaky spying ways, the masters of the most enormously expensive and destructive gadgets in the arsenal of the devil. Just such an agent of the devil was presented to the U.S. public in the late 1990s in the form of the slight Wen Ho Lee, the scientist falsely charged with spying for China. Although he hailed from Taiwan and had spent decades of his life in the United States working at the highly secure national weapons lab in Los Alamos to make our bombs even more destructive, he was the best the hawks could come up with. However, that ploy failed when the case against him totally collapsed and a conservative Reagan-appointed federal judge holding court in Albuquerque, New Mexico, apologized to Wen Ho Lee and set him free.

But "the Chinese are coming" hawks are still beating that drum. The growing Chinese threat was the preoccupation of the neocons before 9/11, and as much as they liked the war on terror after 9/11, they know that those ragtag stateless terror thugs do not possess the panache required for an enemy in a revived Cold War. In their eagerness to build an empire based on an immense U.S. military, they require a formidable nation-state enemy. China is the best candidate to fill that vacancy.

If not the Chinese, then perhaps the Putin-led Russians or some other formidable national power with the wherewithal to provide the sustainable appearance, if not the reality, of a military threat to the United States will justify an enormous U.S defense budget. Without heavy-duty enemies, the kind that have jets, subs, and nukes, to conquer, who's going to want to pay for a Pax Americana?

Chapter 12

THE HUMBLING OF PAX AMERICANA

There is no activity in the private or public sector better insulated from objective criticism than the preparation and conduct of war. Sure, waste may occur, the weapons may not work, even the wrong war may be fought, but the intentions of those claiming to protect the populace from foreign menace are all too easily presumed to be praiseworthy, and suggestions of a more prudent course are scorned. So, too, the very idea that those who advocate for war may also be profiting from it.

As the air-tanker scandal discussed in Chapter 3 reveals, it is difficult to separate the twin dominant impulses driving the bloated military budget: is it a matter of blatant pecuniary greed or a reflection of genuine, if misplaced, concern for shoring up the nation's *security*?

In the case of convicted felon Darleen Druyun, those impulses seem to have been serially in effect. During a long career with the Pentagon, she was highly regarded as one who cared about the cost-effective appropriation of the taxpayers' dollars to the military budget and presumably made many sound decisions in recommending one weapons system and its manufacturer over another. But in her last years on the job, she clearly swung over to the greed column, fattening the receipts for at least one corporation that could ensure lucrative future jobs for herself and her kin through the revolving door into private enterprise.

I doubt that Druyun and the thousands of others who have followed this path, though not necessarily to the point of convictable crime, know exactly where the commitment to the nation's well-being gave way to preoccupation with personal career or wealth. Green-lighting a weapons system can all too easily be justified. The reason is that throughout the process of government military allocation, most of those involved—the Armed Forces brass, the pro-military members of Congress who stack the relevant committees, and the corporate lobbyists— become deeply convinced that all weapons are needed. How can it hurt to have too many planes, ships, and guns? They have talked themselves into believing that when it is a matter of national security, damn the expense.

The exceptions are the "green eyeshade" bean counters in the Pentagon, who take seriously their fiduciary responsibility to use public resources wisely and who were condemned for their opposition to the air-tanker deal in that *Wall Street Journal* column by Richard Perle and Thomas Donnelly. But for the neocon militarists like them, a fervent ideological commitment to a massive military, capable of imposing a Pax Americana on the world, easily trumps any nagging concerns about the efficacy of a particular weapons system.

While Perle had benefited from Boeing's largesse, it is quite possible that his motives in advocating for Boeing's air tanker were pure. Perle most likely was speaking the truth when he stated that he favored the tankers quite apart from the dollar benefits that Boeing had bestowed upon him in that he favored the most expansive of U.S. military force projections, so why not have more tankers?

That certainly is true of his coauthor on the *Wall Street Journal* piece, Thomas Donnelly, who worked for Boeing's main competitor, Lockheed Martin, in the year before he wrote that essay as the company's director of strategic communications and initiatives. In his earlier work experience, Donnelly edited trade journals that catered to the interests of defense corporations, and he had also been rewarded with positions at industry-supported think tanks and with consulting work. But like Perle, he also seems to be a true believer in the cause.

Although originally a disciple of Perle, Donnelly has emerged in his own right as some sort of poet laureate of the neoconservative movement, singing with as strong and clear a voice as any of the neocons the praises of America as the sole superpower obligated to reorder the world. Donnelly is worth reading, for when he describes the opportunities and obligations that await an America in possession of greater military might than the world has ever seen, he leaves no doubt as to just what he means. Given that Donnelly wrote the PNAC manifesto calling for a Pax Americana, his exposition of that doctrine is all the more significant.

In an article he wrote for the American Enterprise Institute on January 31, 2003, Donnelly quoted Paul Kennedy: "Nothing has ever existed like this disparity of power." Donnelly was celebrating what he called the Bush Doctrine, based on a revitalized notion of Pax Americana. Ironically, it also was based on a military power that President Bill Clinton had presided over for eight years as commander in chief and which his neocon critics had roundly condemned as being shriveled by too-tight Pentagon budgets. Again, quoting Kennedy, extolling U.S. power:

The Pax Britannica was run on the cheap, Britain's army was much smaller than European armies, and even the Royal Navy was equal only to the next two navies—right now all the other navies in the world combined could not dent American maritime supremacy. Charlemagne's empire was merely western-European in its reach. The Roman Empire stretched farther afield, but there was another great empire in Persia and a larger one in China. There is, therefore, no comparison.

Donnelly used those words to validate his own politics:

In other words, the fundamental premise of the Bush Doctrine is true: The United States possesses the means—economic, military, diplomatic—to realize its expansive geopolitical purposes. Further, and especially in light of the domestic political reaction to the attacks of September 11, the victory in Afghanistan and the remarkable skill demonstrated by President Bush in focusing national attention, it is equally true that Americans possess the requisite political willpower to pursue an expansive strategy.

He was right, until he was wrong. Donnelly wrote that ode to the new imperialism seven weeks before the Bush-ordered invasion of Iraq, and while the "requisite willpower" of the American people did last as long as the public believed in the rationalizations for the war. But as Abraham Lincoln cautioned about the inability to fool all the people all the time, the public eventually caught on. The Iraq war proved the death knell for the neocon putsch, and within three years, the leading neocons in the Defense Department, beginning with Perle, but then Douglas Feith, Paul Wolfowitz, and finally Donald Rumsfeld, were all gone. So, too, was not just their power to set the agenda but also what had appealed to some as the fresh charm of their arrogance. Their proclamations had made for great rhetoric before Bush assumed office, but not for long after, when their prophetic power would come to be tested by facts on the ground.

It is Donnelly who is credited with actually writing "Rebuilding America's Defenses," the defining manifesto of the Project for the New American Century, which Cheney and Rumsfeld backed and which predicted the George W. Bush doctrine. It is curious that the title, as does the Pentagon itself, continues to rely on the notion that the U.S. military posture is based on defense, when in fact what is outlined in the document is a strategy of deliberate offense, even when there are no formidable enemies in sight. As with empire builders before them, the goal is to exert a power over the world so pervasive that no rival will ever rise to challenge its dominance. As Donnelly wrote in the PNAC manifesto, "The American peace has proven itself peaceful, stable, and durable. Yet no moment in international politics can be frozen in time: even a global Pax Americana will not preserve itself." What is required is a "foundation" of "unquestioned U.S. military preeminence."

In one of his business activities, Donnelly runs a guide service that takes executives and other leaders on a crash-course tour of U.S. battle sites to garner the lessons of leadership. The image of the U.S. Cavalry seems always foremost in his discussion of the United States' foreign policy. In an article he coauthored for the American Enterprise Institute in 2003, he wrote: "In sum, the strategic imperative of patrolling the perimeter of the Pax Americana is transforming the U.S. military, and those few other forces capable or willing of standing alongside, into the cavalry of a global, liberal international order. Like the cavalry of the Old West, their job is one part warrior and one part policeman—both of which are entirely within the tradition of the American military."

The war against Iraq, which Donnelly and the other neocons strongly advocated, represented in their view just such a charge of the cavalry, and the U.S. military certainly performed powerfully in its part-warrior role against that bizarrely unmatched enemy that lacked any of the lethal weapons of mass destruction that the neocons used to justify the strike on Iraq as a serious military confrontation. But what Donnelly and the others got totally wrong was the difficulty of playing the part-policeman role.

As described by Donnelly in that January 31, 2003, article entitled "The Underpinnings of the Bush Doctrine," posted on the site of the American Enterprise Institute for Public Policy Research shortly before the invasion of Iraq, the upcoming task of transforming the military defeat of Saddam Hussein into a Pax Americana for the entire Mideast region was presented as not much of a problem.

The new Bush Doctrine, which they had sold to George W. Bush, "represents a reversal of course from Clinton-era policies in regard to the uses of U.S. power and, especially, military force." That's for sure, but it also represented a break from that of all U.S. Cold War presidents, including Bush's father, whose administration witnessed the end of Soviet communism. It is a total break, although Donnelly is at pains to find historical antecedents because it is built on a notion of unquestioned supremacy of the United States in the post–Cold War world.

The reality that Donnelly and the other neocons played down

is that other nations still have forces; the Russians still possess a nuclear arsenal equivalent to our own, along with the means to enforce the old Cold War threat of mutual assured destruction of each of our societies. Others, as he concedes, even some rogue nations, had also developed this nuclear force equalizer.

But the more serious error, as became clearly evident after the failed occupation of Iraq, was that military power in itself cannot ensure a regime change positive to one's purposes. Reading Donnelly's piece, written before the invasion, makes it clear that he foresaw no such pitfall in the way of imposing his Pax Americana on Iraq and the region:

> Blessed now with a global balance heavily weighted in favor of the United States, the Bush administration has declared itself ready to remove the rogue regimes and terrorists it regards as uniquely dangerous. For Americans, normal power calculations of "threats" and "opportunities" have been colored by an abiding faith in a set of political principles believed to have universal application. Americans have come to regard the exercise of their power as not simply a force for national greatness but for human liberty.

Certainly some Americans have thought that over the years, and others, most often a clear majority, have leaned to an isolationist view. Even in the aftermath of 9/11, the vast majority was willing to support Bush in invading Iraq, but it was not on the basis of America spreading liberty. On the contrary, the Bush administration was taking great pains to fabricate a defensive case that Iraq possessed weapons of mass destruction and, because of ties to bin Laden, would pass them on to terrorists. President Bush, who had been elected on a platform that scorned nation building, including some of the foreign commitments of U.S. forces under Clinton, did not suddenly reverse himself and make the case for rebuilding Iraq in our image. But, knowingly or not, his invasion of Iraq took him inevitably down that slippery slope.

That part Donnelly did get right: "having, at last, determined to reform the politics of the greater Middle East, we will find it difficult and dangerous to stop with half measures." It is only from this point of view that the abject losses of neocon-led policies in the world, particularly in Iraq, have paradoxically produced a victory for them, if not their nation. To be cynical about it, dragging the United States into a quagmire elsewhere creates an alternative reality. One administration insider famously told journalist and author Ron Suskind in an October 17, 2004, *New York Times Magazine* article, "We're an empire now, and when we act, we create our own reality. And while you're studying that reality—judiciously, as you will—we'll act again, creating other new realities, which you can study, too, and that's how things will sort out. We're history's actors . . . and you, all of you, will be left to just study what we do."

In the neocon worldview, one succeeds by failing because even when the initial intervention cannot be defended, refusing to pull out is presented as noble in the service of national honor, obligation to the fallen soldiers, or perceptions of American power.

The latter is a card that neocons like Donnelly particularly love to play:

> The preservation of today's Pax Americana rests
> upon both actual military strength and the percep-
> tion of strength. The variety of victories scored by
> U.S. forces since the end of the Cold War is testa-
> ment to both the futility of directly challenging

the United States and the desire of its enemies to keep poking and prodding to find a weakness in the American global order.

But what if the opposite is true? What if it is the very perception of that strength, the supreme power of that Pax Americana, that feeds the passions of the enemies? After all, as discussed earlier, the Cold War ended after the U.S. defeat in Vietnam and not because of a U.S. victory there. Then there was the defeat of the United States in Iran over the hostage crisis. No less a believer in U.S. military power than Ronald Reagan negotiated arms sales to Iran and then an alliance with Saddam Hussein to contain the ayatollahs.

Feeding all of that opposition to the United States, and leading to the recruitment of al Qaeda terrorists, as is well documented in the 9/11 Commission Report, was the argument that the all-powerful U.S. could be held responsible for all that goes wrong in the world. Certainly that has been the problem with the U.S. occupation of Iraq, where problems arising from long-standing ethnic and religious rivalries, a dilapidated infrastructure, and endemic civic corruption are all attributed to the U.S. reconstruction.

The assumption of the neocons and a far larger circle of defense hawks is that enemies arise, as do new viruses, festering diseases called communism, the Mafia, narco-terrorists, and most recently Islamo-fascists. These are presumed to be completely self-generating pathogens that feed on the healthy tissues of democracies; they hate us for what we are, as Bush put it, with the assumption being that what we are is virtuous. Surely, there is an element of truth to this view. There are movements that are fueled by slogans or even full-blown ideologies that are poisonously racist, anti-Semitic, ethnically chauvinistic, undemocratic, and otherwise divisive and oppressive, but the assumption that this offers a clear linear trajectory of the growth of a terrorist threat is belied by a reading of the evidence collected in the 9/11 Commission Report.

To Donnelly and the other neocons, the "war on terrorism" is, as he puts it in "The Underpinnings of the Bush Doctrine":

> in truth, not a global war on all terrorist organizations—so far, the FARC in Columbia and the Irish Republican Army seemed to have escaped much attention from the Bush administration—but principally upon "Islamism," that violent political movement antipathetic to modernity and to the West, and especially to their expression through American power. The motivating core of this movement appears to be more "Arab" than "pan-Islamic," and often stems from the Saudi-funded spread of Wahhabism. It is like communism in that it is, in some measure, an ideologically motivated international political movement, though it relies upon the means of military weakness—terrorism—where the Soviet Union deployed great tank armies and nuclear arsenals.

That one paragraph wonderfully summarizes the contradictions and ignorance at the heart of the U.S. military buildup in response to 9/11. First, given that terrorism arises out of military weakness, one must question the investment of trillions of dollars in continuing to build up precisely the arsenal that the former Soviets no longer deploy, and which the terrorists don't have. But in that statement is also the need to identify the current scourge with the past one—both presumed to be international and driven in a linear, expansionist way by the force of ideology. Hence the need for a rival Pax Americana ideology.

But then how does one explain why the most steadfast ally of the United States in the Mideast, outside of Israel, for the past half century has been Saudi Arabia, which has been the main funding source for this anti-U.S. Wahhabism? Didn't the United States save Saudi Arabia from being overrun by a fellow Arab state as recently as the first Gulf War? And just how did this Wahhabism get to be so intrinsically anti-American, when it was our ally in recruiting what Ronald Reagan praised as "freedom fighters" to do battle with the Soviets in Afghanistan? Or Chechnya? Or Bosnian Muslims, whom Clinton supported against Christian Serb aggressors?

The harsh facts as outlined by the 9/11 Commission Report, meticulously detailing the planning of that attack, make it all too clear that the United States was not the inevitable target. Nor does it support the view that they attacked us, as Bush insisted, because "they hate our freedoms." Bin Laden was our ally, preoccupied with defeating the godless communists who were oppressing Muslims in Afghanistan and Chechnya. He became obsessed with the United States not over the state of freedom in our country, which certainly hadn't changed qualitatively since we were on the same side in Afghanistan, but rather over the stationing of U.S. troops in Saudi Arabia at the time of the first Gulf War.

Much more is known about the state of mind of Khalid Sheikh Mohammed, the mastermind of 9/11, if one is to believe the results of his interrogation after being captured by the United States, as documented by the 9/11 Commission. KSM, as he is referred to in the report, was the beneficiary of an American college education, first at a small Baptist school called Chowan College and then at North Carolina Agricultural and

Technical State University. He graduated in 1986, and, as the Commission states: "Although he apparently did not attract attention for extreme Islamist beliefs or activities while in the United States, KSM plunged into the anti-Soviet Afghan jihad soon after graduating college." Clearly, whatever hatred KSM harbored for the American brand of freedom that Bush argues drives the terrorists was secondary to his antipathy toward the Soviets who had invaded Muslim Afghanistan.

According to the 9/11 Commission's findings, it was not KSM's experience with freedom as a student in the United States that would later inspire his hostility toward this country, but rather a specific aspect of U.S. foreign policy: support of Israel. There is not one instance cited anywhere of his having objected to our freedom or any other manifestation of our way of life as he experienced it. As the 9/11 Commission Report states, "By his own account, KSM's animus toward the United States stemmed not from his experience there as a student, but rather from his violent disagreement with U.S. foreign policy favoring Israel."

Even the four key jihadists, the Hamburg cell, including lead hijacker Mohamed Atta, had the Russians in Chechnya as their intended target upon committing to jihad—not the Americans in New York and Washington—until a chance encounter with an al Qaeda associate on a train changed their focus. Referring to the Hamburg Four, the 9/11 Commission reported:

> The available evidence indicates that in 1999, Atta, Binalshibh, Shehhi, and Jarrah decided to fight in Chechnya against the Russians. According to Binalshibh, a chance meeting on a train in Germany caused the group to travel to Afghanistan instead. An individual named Khalid al Masri

approached Binalshibh and Shehhi (because they were Arabs with beards, Binalshibh thinks) and struck up a conversation about jihad in Chechnya.

Later, they called Masri, who put them in touch with an al Qaeda operative known to the German police, who told them that at the moment it was difficult to go directly to Chechnya, but that they should head to Afghanistan for training and then on to their intended target area. It was in Afghanistan that they met bin Laden and were recruited to train as pilots in the U.S. hijacking venture.

Atta then became the leader of the hijackers, and he too presents a challenge to the overly simplistic explanations of Islamo-fascism driven by Saudi Wahhabism. The son of an Egyptian attorney, he was not considered fanatically religious and seemed to apply himself seriously as a student at Cairo University, where he graduated, and later in Hamburg, where he mastered the German language and did well in his studies. While he is reported to have voiced "virulently anti-Semitic and anti-American opinions," he also condemned the anti-Israel governments of the Arab world: "To him, Saddam Hussein was an American stooge set up to give Washington an excuse to intervene in the Middle East."

That was before the U.S. invasion in response to 9/11, and it would suggest that the neocon-inspired U.S. interventionist policy played directly into the hands of those attempting to recruit future Mohamed Attas sufficiently enraged to want to attack the United States. Certainly it would indicate that the Pax Americana military power that Donnelly was celebrating is at best irrelevant to countering terrorists like Atta. After all, they were attracted to jihad as a response to Soviet military power, which was certainly manifested through the sort of high-tech war-fighting machines at which the United States threw money after 9/11. Yet if Soviet jets, submarines, and even the threat of nuclear weapons were ineffective in defeating the jihadists, why would ours have a different impact?

The reliance on sophisticated modern weaponry, the mighty armada of Pax Americana that Donnelly and the other neocons celebrate, is largely beside the point in fighting what has been called fourth-generation or asymmetrical warfare. Insurgents can always hide among the general population, and the use of massive firepower is counterproductive, causing collateral damage that alienates the citizenry. The harsh lesson of the Afghanistan and Iraq wars for the United States is that the much-vaunted "shock and awe" strategy of relying on cutting-edge precision-guided bombing doesn't cut it. Asymmetrical warfare is inevitably messy, requiring troops to be on the ground and vulnerable. The big push in the 2008 spending budget was for better armed vehicles, not faster planes.

That was the lesson that Israel learned after its failed war with Hezbollah in Lebanon, when it went through a major reorganization of its forces in its five-year plan called the Tefen 2012 report. As the Jewish Institute for National Security Affairs (JINSA) reported: "The Israel Defense Forces (IDF) has reprioritized its acquisition schedule for years to come as a consequence of lessons learned from the summer 2006 battles with Hezbollah. . . . The new plan will have the IDF concentrate on bolstering manpower over technology."

The problem for U.S. warmongers is that their notion of American hegemony was based on exactly the opposite assumption: that technology could substitute for manpower. The lesson of Vietnam, and now of Iraq and Afghanistan, is that the citizens of a representative republic will use the vote to restrain politicians who engage in prolonged ground warfare leading to increased fatalities and injuries. The post-Vietnam strategy had been to create an electronic battlefield in which relatively few soldiers would be put at risk. That hasn't happened and won't ever happen when the battle is against locally based insurgents.

In Iraq, the U.S. hawks' assumption that a low American casualty "shock and awe" air campaign would create the conditions for an easy regime change to a new Iraq and Middle East produced exactly the opposite outcome. The invasion was a great success, and the "peaceful" aftermath was a disaster. In the end, a modicum of stability can only be purchased in the region with a large and expensive troop commitment to an on-the-ground campaign. That is why by 2007 the budget for the Iraq and Afghanistan wars reached $200 billion, primarily to support the troops, and high-tech acquisitions seemed increasingly irrelevant.

The fact that the vaunted Israel Defense Forces, considered perhaps the most effective military in the world in fighting asymmetrical wars, has reversed course is sobering. At a time when the United States continues to put faith and enormous sums of money into a new generation of weaponry, the Israeli reversal deserves notice. That was particularly true with regard to the most expensive item in the U.S. buildup: the projected $300 billion program to build the multiservice F-35 fighter. The F-35 program has been sold to Congress in part on the assumption that other nations were on board as investors and future customers for the plane, but in a stunning rebuke to those plans, Israel cut back its order of the Lockheed Martin aircraft from one hundred to twenty-five. Instead, Israel will rely on the F-16s it already owns, which raises the question of why the United States needs the new plane when it, too, has plenty of the older ones which seem better suited for the close-in air-to-ground support required for wars of the future.

The problem with those wars, basically intrusions into the messy affairs of others, is that the military effort likewise becomes messy and drains away support at home, whether the motive for the military intervention is cast as humanitarian or sovereign in its ambition. That is the lesson learned by every imperial power, and most nations that have tried it in the past—Japan, Russia, France, England, Germany, and Spain on the short list—have given up the game. Occupation doesn't pay; it didn't for Pax Britannica, and it won't for Pax Americana.

Chapter 13

BUT IS IT GOOD FOR THE JEWS?

If Pax Americana does not pay, why is the United States in Iraq as the first chapter in a new imperial era? In their carefully researched and thoughtfully considered book, John J. Mearsheimer and Stephen M. Walt provide an answer that is also the title of their book: *The Israel Lobby*. The authors write that "Many Americans believe that this was a 'war for oil' (or for corporations like Halliburton) but there is little direct evidence to support this claim and considerable evidence that casts doubt on it." They do not provide that evidence, nor do they deal adequately with the inconvenient fact that the former CEO of Halliburton became the U.S. vice president who led the charge to war. Or that Halliburton's formerly bankrupt subsidiary, KBR, got $16 billion in government contracts for work in Iraq and Afghanistan in a two-year period.

Nor do they even consider the possibility that the war was pursued as a means of justifying an immense U.S. military buildup in the wake of 9/11 that would provide "better targets," to use Rumsfeld's phrase, and hence justification for revving up the production of Cold War–era weapons. Indeed, as is the convention with most academic national security analysts, they do not even refer to the military-industrial complex as a concept.

What they do instead is project a more limited, but no less all-encompassing, force behind the invasion of Iraq: the Israel lobby. In their chapter on the drive to go to war with Iraq, the authors "argue that the war was motivated at least in good part by a desire to make Israel more secure," and place the blame on the neoconservatives, who are assumed to be preoccupied with Israel's security. As I have discussed in detail, there is no question about the important role of the neocons in the entire military buildup after the collapse of the Soviet Union and certainly in the decision to invade Iraq, but to suggest, as *The Israel Lobby* does, that their defining motive is the protection of Israel is quite wrong in my view. The authors simply lump the neocons in as part of a broader Israel lobby, writing that "a proper account of the lobby's role in encouraging the war is ultimately a question of evidence, and there is considerable evidence that Israel and pro-Israel groups—especially the neoconservatives— played important roles in the decision to invade."

What follows is an exploration of connections between the neocons and Israel that manages to ignore their ties to Kuwait, United Arab Emirates, Saudi Arabia, Turkey, Pakistan, and other countries as well as their connection to the U.S. defense industry. The book assumes that the neocons are in the service of Israel, rather than entertaining the possibility that they've ensnared Israel in the service of their own agenda. As much as the book insists that there is a bond strong enough to inspire the lust for war, it oddly fails to examine the alleged alliance between the neocons and Israel in much detail. What is the attraction or allegiance at work here? Surely it is not that many of them are Jewish because, as is pointed out in *The Israel Lobby*, opinion polls show Jews were less supportive of the Iraq war than non-Jews.

The best source for measuring Jewish opinion is the American Jewish Committee's annual survey. That poll for 2003, nine months after the Iraq invasion, found that 54 percent of Jews disapproved of the war with Iraq, and an equal number criticized Bush's handling of the war on terrorism. By November 2007, the annual survey found that 67 percent of Jews thought the United States should have stayed out of Iraq, and 59 percent disapproved of the way the U.S. government was handling the campaign against terrorism.

Is it that the Jewish neocons are more closely identified with their religion than is the larger Jewish population? Even casual contemplation of this crowd would show that rationale to be questionable. There is no evidence that they are particularly observant of the strictures of the religion, and indeed Paul Wolfowitz, their most prominent member pushing the Iraq war, had parted from his Jewish wife and was seeing a Muslim woman, Shaha Ali Riza, during the run-up to the war and well into his time after the Pentagon when he headed the World Bank. Wolfowitz was forced to resign his position in May 2007 after it was revealed that he had brokered a lucrative deal for Riza to move from the World Bank in order to spare himself the embarrassment of a conflict of interest in supervising his paramour. These folks may be in it for the political cause, but the money isn't bad. Wolfowitz was paid $400,000 a year at the World Bank job, his reward for bungling Iraq, and Riza got a $193,590 tax-free job at the State Department as her consolation prize.

That one of the key people whom Wolfowitz trusted in the buildup to invasion, again according to media accounts, was a Muslim Arab who was also a neoconservative with strong Mideast policy views seemed to debunk the notion that feelings of Jewish identity drove Wolfowitz to support the war. It is a serious omission that the authors of *The Israel Lobby* never reference Riza as a possible source of inspiration for Wolfowitz's Iraq views, when she was in fact deeply involved in planning for the Iraq war and its aftermath.

After the toppling of Saddam Hussein, the Pentagon finally woke up to questions concerning the rule of the country they occupied, and Douglas Feith ordered defense contractor SAIC to pay Riza to come up with some answers. Feith reported to Wolfowitz and, like his boss, is said to be part of the Israel lobby, but both relied heavily upon exiles from the Muslim world in the formulation of Iraq policy. None was more important than the now infamous Ahmed Chalabi, an Iraqi Shiite whom the CIA had long mistrusted for his ties to Tehran and later accused of passing U.S. secrets to Iran. Clearly, while some of the neocons were Jewish, they moved easily in a wide circle of people who were not Jewish and for whom the well-being of Israel was hardly a central concern.

Most of the leading neocons who are Jewish do not, in general, come out of a Zionist tradition. Indeed, if one is to generalize, their roots are planted much more firmly in the anti-Zionist Trotskyite left, as indicated by the prior political history of the founders of neoconservatism, Irving Kristol, father of Bill, Norman Podhoretz, and Midge Dector. These are people who came to support Israel not because of any desire to abandon their Greenwich Village and Georgetown homes and build a kibbutz in the forlorn deserts of the Mideast.

The academic progenitors of the neocons, the University of Chicago's Leo Strauss, Allan Bloom, and Albert Wohlstetter, were hardly preoccupied with Israel or even very interested in that nation. Their vision was global: the desire for the United States to reject the moral relativism that had led the West to coddle Hitler and instead assert the predominant moral force that the rest of the world sorely needed. Their enemy was the "evil" that festered when otherwise well-intentioned people "ignored," "appeased," or in any way "accommodated" it. In the Cold War enemy of international communism they had their villain, and its elimination, rather than containment, was the goal. To the degree that Israel, an admired and militarily tough democracy, was a useful ally in that enterprise, it would be more than welcome, but the well-being of the Jewish state was hardly the central obsession.

That essential take was revealed early on in the doctoral dissertation that Wolfowitz wrote under Wohlstetter's tutelage at the University of Chicago. As James Mann describes in his very important book on the neocons and Bush, *Rise of the Vulcans*, Wolfowitz's work from that time was the opposite of Israel-centric. Wohlstetter, a major defense intellectual, had become properly obsessed with the danger of the proliferation of nuclear weapons in general and to the Mideast in particular. As Mann describes it, in the 1960s Wohlstetter became concerned about U.S. plans to aid in the building of nuclear-powered desalination plants alongside Israel's border with Egypt and Jordan. It was the old atoms-for-peace idea, using nuclear power to supply much-needed water to the three nations at a low cost. But Wohlstetter was concerned that the plutonium generated in the process could find its way eventually into nuclear weapons. He had brought back documents in Hebrew from Israel and, when he learned that Wolfowitz could read the language, encouraged him to write a dissertation on the subject.

Wolfowitz did, and his work supported Wohlstetter's opposition to the program. As Mann explains:

> What seems especially noteworthy, in retro-
> spect, is that Wolfowitz's warnings about nuclear

proliferation applied at the time to Israel as much as to the Arab states. Wolfowitz specifically argued against an Israeli nuclear weapon. The fundamental point is that any Israeli nuclear force would have to depend on relatively simple delivery systems, which would be vulnerable even to conventional attack. . . . An Israeli nuclear threat against Arab cities would weaken Israel's conventional military position by cutting her off from friendly countries in the West, and by encouraging, if not forcing, the Soviet Union to intervene more actively on behalf of the Arabs. . . . Israeli nuclear weapons would push the Arabs into a desperate attempt to acquire nuclear weapons, if not from the Soviet Union, then at a later date from China or on their own.

How brilliantly prescient, yet after Israel did develop nuclear weapons in the early 1970s and other rival nations attempted to follow suit, Wolfowitz did not criticize Israel for having taken the step.

I offer this background only as an illustration of the thinking of key neocons, who are too often driven by concerns other than the prerogatives demanded by the Israeli government to assume that they are in some integral way a simple addendum to the Israel lobby. If Israel had been inclined, or permitted by its neighbors, to be a dovish state aligned with the views of what was then called the nonaligned Third World movement, which a considerable number of Israelis favored, then it would have been of scant interest to the emerging neocons. Or if the Soviets had followed a policy, as did the United States, of supporting both Israel and its neighbors, pitting one against the other, then

Israel would have been more independent in the Cold War and perhaps criticized by the neocons.

No, Israel became important to the neocons because that nation lined up with their own view of the need for a heavily militarized United States during the Cold War. It didn't have to be that way. The Soviet Union, still led by Joseph Stalin no less, was the second nation after the U.S. to recognize the new state. The Soviets, through their Czechoslovakian surrogates, had supplied arms to the Israelis fighting to establish their state. But the Soviets decided that their great power interests were better served by lining up with the Arab countries in order to coax Third World independence from the U.S. during the Cold War. That was bitterly disappointing to many Israelis, particularly in the leftist-oriented and idealistic kibbutz movement that provided much of the officer corps. But they were betrayed by the Soviets, who proceeded to arm Egypt and other Arab states, so the Israelis turned to the United States for the military arsenal they felt they needed for their state's survival.

Thus was born the notion of Israel as the land-based aircraft carrier in the Mideast, standing alone against hostile Arab countries tempted to play the Soviets against the Americans, as did Nasser in Egypt and Assad in Syria. When Israel's leaders lined up with the West in the first Suez War against Egypt in 1956, they ensured the support of all American hawks, with the exception of those who were too anti-Semitic to warmly embrace the Jewish nation. But for most hawks, the first Suez war was decisive because it aligned Israel with England and France, a participant in the battle to ensure Western control of the Suez Canal and through it control of Mideast oil.

While the authors of *The Israel Lobby* cavalierly dismiss the argument that the Iraq war was about oil in a matter of a few paragraphs and without serious evidence, it is impossible to understand the politics of the Mideast and the U.S. role in the region without reference to that scarce commodity. Oil was always a huge prize, whether it was in the CIA-engineered coup against Mohammed Mossadegh, the secular elected leader of Iran, or his replacement, the invented Shah of Shahs, Reza Pahlavi. The Shah first presented himself as pro-Israel, and Israel returned the favor. So much so that the Shah's dreaded secret police, the Savak, were trained by Israel, and the sordid involvement of this much-ballyhooed democratic outpost in the Mideast in the oppressive structure that maintained the Shah in power goes a long way to explain the rise of a fiercely anti-Israel Islamic movement in that country. But by the end of his reign, the Shah was no longer thought to be so valuable by the United States, because in order to pay for all of the military equipment, luxury hotels, and other junk that U.S. hustlers had sold him, he had to jack up the price of oil. The Shah reinvented himself and OPEC to demand a higher price for oil, which had been historically kept low compared to the cost of goods bought from the industrialized nations. He soon lost the fervid support of his Western patrons and his grip on power.

After the Shah's fall, Iran became the bastion of anti-U.S. and anti-Israel sentiment as well as the major financial supporter and arms supplier for insurgent movements hostile to Israel in Lebanon, Gaza, and throughout the region. What seeming irony that the U.S. invasion of Iraq vastly increased the power of the fiercely anti-Israel ayatollahs of Iran by eliminating their arch secular rival, Saddam Hussein. The latter, it should be noted, was by that point far less active in supporting anti-Israel groups than was Iran. It is also a matter of fact that Iran had embarked on a nuclear program that could conceivably produce a weapon threatening Israel's existence, while Iraq had no such thing.

By overthrowing Saddam, who drew his support from Iraq's

Sunni minority, the United States, following the lead of the presumably pro-Israel neocons, put the future of Iraq under the control of the Shia majority. Shia militants had been training in Iran for decades and continued to be supported by their fellow religious fanatics during years of fighting the U.S. occupation. To believe that this disastrous outcome for Israel was simply an error in judgment by the neocons assumes that they are extraordinarily ignorant of Mideast reality, which they are not.

With friends like the neocons, Israel doesn't need enemies. What the neocons wanted most of all was a robust U.S. military presence in the world, and the Likud wing of the Israeli political spectrum, with which they were closely allied, afforded them some lobbying ammunition within the United States and some "democratic" cover for an imperial invasion. The use of Israel extended to making the case that Saddam was another Hitler and that those who chose diplomacy and the United Nations over preemptive U.S. war were appeasers in the model of England's Neville Chamberlain.

The Israelis are quite willing to play loose with that argument. In the run-up to the war, as *The Israel Lobby* cites, a number of Israeli leaders advocated taking out Saddam. But it is simply wrong to state that Israel was leading the charge when in fact the government was quite consistently holding the position that Iran, and not Iraq, was the main threat to peace in the region, and that overthrowing Saddam might, as it has, very much strengthen Iran's power. It is certainly true, as the authors of *The Israel Lobby* state, that "Israel's concerns about Iran never led it to undertake a significant effort to halt the march to war" with Iraq, but that is a very different charge—indeed at odds with the claim that Israel and its U.S. lobby instigated the war.

The record is quite clear that a number of key neocons, who had strong ties with the Likud and other right-wing

Israelis, had attempted to merge Israel's need for security with their own fantasy of an American superpower built to spread democratic values throughout the world.

That was the vision of the 1996 "Clean Break" report some leading neocons wrote for the incoming right-wing Israeli government headed by Benjamin Netanyahu. The report, a repudiation of Israel's founders, urged a fundamental break with "labor Zionism, which for 70 years has dominated the Zionist movement." Directed by Richard Perle and coauthored by other leading neocons including Douglas Feith and David Wurmser, the report attacked Israel's social welfare economy as well as the government's past efforts at land-for-peace negotiations with the Palestinians. It called for a strategy of preemptive attacks against the Palestinians and neighboring Arab states including a "focus on removing Saddam Hussein from power in Iraq." There was a revealing naïveté in the paper suggesting that liberating the Shia from Saddam's grip would somehow undermine Shia-led Iran and the Hezbollah movement in Lebanon, when in fact just the opposite occurred. It is also true that in the aftermath of the failed Iraq occupation, the United States and Israel have returned to exactly the land-for-peace negotiations that Perle and his colleagues were rejecting.

Unquestionably, Perle was influential in getting the Bush administration to go to war, and Feith, who became undersecretary of defense, named Wurmser to a secret Pentagon intelligence unit that cherry-picked the data making the case for war. The *Washington Post* reported on September 4, 2004, that Wurmser and Feith were questioned by the FBI in a case involving the passage of classified information to Ahmed Chalabi and/ or the American Israel Public Affairs Committee (AIPAC).

It also is true that some of the neocons got very excited about the prospect of Ahmed Chalabi, the leader of the exile group the Iraqi National Congress, which the CIA funded. In their eagerness to believe in the case for intervention, they bought the Chalabi line that Iraq, without Saddam, not only would embrace democracy but Israel as well, despite his close ties to Iran and his own checkered history in the region, including being wanted on bank fraud charges in Jordan. Even better, he would give them oil. Chalabi told L. Marc Zell, an Israeli who was Feith's former law partner, that he would rebuild the pipeline from Haifa to Mosul. (Imagine having to protect that pipeline.)

What a deal. "This was precisely what pro-Israel proponents of regime change wanted to hear," Mearsheimer and Walt write, "so they backed Chalabi in return." Maybe some pro-Israel proponents were that naive, but it is difficult to believe that Israeli intelligence, reputed to be the best in the world, would get snookered by Chalabi. At the very least they would have known, as did the neocons, that U.S. intelligence agencies thought he was a con man at best and an Iranian agent at worst. Surely if the Israeli lobby in the United States is as closely tied to the Israeli government as is claimed, it would have been forewarned not to get too excited about Chalabi's qualifications to lead a liberated Iraq.

The Iran connection would have been most disturbing, and whatever pro-Iraq invasion signals may have come from Israel, their main concern was the threat from Iran. As Lawrence Wilkerson, chief of staff in Colin Powell's State Department, put it: "The Israelis tried their best to persuade us that we were focused on the wrong enemy [and that] they were very leery of destroying the balance of power in the Middle East. But once they understood that we were going to war, come hell or high water, they weren't going to get on the wrong side of the president of the United States." Now, he said that in an interview with the *New Yorker*'s Jeffrey Goldberg after the war was going badly and when everyone, Powell included, was trying to distance himself or herself from the debacle. It is also true that once the war commenced, the Israelis went gangbusters in their all-out support.

At the hawkish American Israel Public Affairs Committee convention two weeks into the Iraq war, leading Israeli spokespersons showed up in Washington to warmly embrace the Bush administration while undermining the war's detractors. That support continued uncritically, and four years later, Israeli Prime Minister Ehud Olmert addressed the AIPAC convention in Washington by video and told the assembled audience, which included many U.S. senators and members of the House, that they should be cheerleaders for Bush's adventure in Iraq. "Those who are concerned for Israel's security," Olmert advised, "should recognize the need for American success in Iraq." However, even at that moment of support for the U.S. invasion, he went on to state the primacy of the Iranian threat: "Any outcome that will not help America's strength and would, in the eyes of the people in the region, undercut America's ability to deal effectively with the threat posed by the Iranian regime will be very negative."

Whatever the rhetoric coming from the Israeli lobby and the AIPAC convention, the American Jewish community, presumably its most accessible audience, was not swayed. Initial Jewish support for the war, registering at 56 percent in one poll, was, if anything, less enthusiastic than among non-Jews, and by 2007, almost three-quarters of the Jewish population opposed the Bush policy. That's a considerably higher ratio than 56 percent of the total public. Additionally, a vastly disproportionate number of prominent voices critical of the conduct of the war and the occupation came from Jews. These figures are not significant, *The Israel Lobby* authors would argue, because the key pro-Israel organizations have such a fatal stranglehold on Congress. AIPAC's campaign contributions and influence over the media, it seems, hold more power than the votes of individual Jews in elections.

There is no question about the effectiveness of pro-Israel organizations in garnering support for weapons, to the tune of $3 billion a year, and other knee-jerk support for Israel from the U.S. Congress. But support for the American invasion and occupation of Iraq, even assuming that Israel favored such a position, does not seem to have been manifested. *The Israel Lobby* singles out Congressman Henry Waxman, the Democrat from a heavily Jewish Los Angeles district, as one of the most "ardent defenders of Israel" in the Congress. Yet while it is true that Waxman, along with the overwhelming majority of his colleagues, voted for the original war authorization, he has since been one of the toughest critics of the Bush administration's conduct of the Iraq war and occupation.

No member of Congress has been more effective in skewering the claims of the neocons and the rest of the "defense lobby," as opposed to the "Israel lobby," than Waxman, first as the ranking Democrat and, since the 2006 election, as chair of the House Oversight Committee. In that capacity, he has been the principle bête noire of Halliburton, one of the top profiteers from the Iraq war.

The difference between the defense and Israel lobbies is a critical one, because while their interests occasionally overlap, most often they do not. A case in point is the administration's plan to sell $20 billion in arms to Saudi Arabia. That's one deal the defense lobby very much wanted, and yes, to get it through Congress it was necessary to force U.S. taxpayers to shell out $30 billion for Israel. The tail that is Israel gets attention, but the dog, the U.S. military machine, does the wagging.

Whatever the effectiveness of the band of organizations, led by AIPAC, that lobby for Israel's interests, it is a serious error to simply lump them in with the neocons and assume that Israel and its American allies played a decisive role in getting the United States into the Iraq war. Even if one assumes, incorrectly, that the Israel lobby had that power, one would also have to assume an extraordinary degree of stupidity on the part of the Mossad for the Israeli government to not have known full well that the consequences of the Iraq invasion would prove disastrous for Israel's security. A more likely conspiracy theory would feature Iranian agents, led by Ahmed Chalabi, hoodwinking their neocon allies in Washington to topple Saddam. That theory at least predicts the outcome that occurred: Shiites trained in Iran were put in control of Iraq and the influence of the ayatollahs of Tehran extended from Beirut, through Gaza, and on to Baghdad.

Clear writing on the putative Israeli role in getting the United States to invade Iraq was supplied by Joel Beinin, a professor of Middle East Studies at Stanford, along with Mitchell Plitnick and Cecilie Surasky, two leaders of the dovish but certainly pro-Israel Jewish Voice for Peace. In their article "Did Israel Lead the U.S. into the War on Iraq?" published on JVP's Web site, the three authors don't dispute that the Sharon government and most Israelis favored attacking Iraq and that "Israelis operating outside of the Mossad" worked with the CIA to produce the "evidence" supporting the case for invasion. They continued: "But all of this is a far cry from proving that this was a 'war for Israel,'" they argue, correctly pointing out that not only was the war disastrous for Israel, as they and many Israelis had predicted, but that it betrayed a key tenet of the "Clean Break" paper that neocons Richard Perle, Douglas Feith, and others had written for Netanyahu:

> The "Clean Break" paper, which is the corner-
> stone of the "war for Israel" theory, focuses on the

idea of Israel as an independent actor. Where toppling Saddam is one point among many, promoting
an independently-acting Israel is a major theme of
the paper. Although constant lobbying to maintain
and even increase aid to Israel is a permanent face
of Middle East politics in America, the Israeli right,
for whom the "Clean Break" paper was written, has
always sought to move away from American aid so
that Israel could act on its own, without having to
worry about Washington's reaction.

Beinin, Plitnick, and Surasky go on to point out the obvious but overlooked fact that, even if one dismisses the president
as a figurehead, the neocons were hardly leading folks like
Dick Cheney and Donald Rumsfeld, their omnipresent bosses,
around by the nose. Those two

were the clear ringleaders beating the drums
for war on Iraq. They may define America's "interests" differently from most of us, but do we really
believe that they have put the interests of Israel
before what they see as American interests? And, if
protection of Israel was not the prime motivation
for the war, then what American interests were
thought of as being served by it? Oil is both the
obvious and correct answer; specifically, American
control over the region's oil resources, which also
motivates many policymakers' support for Israel.

Of course the fact that Iraq contains the second most significant pool of the most coveted raw material in the world
is very important, particularly since the reliability of Saudi

Arabia as a U.S. ally had been undermined by the 9/11 attacks, in which fifteen of the nineteen hijackers were Saudi citizens in good standing. It is absurd for those like the authors of *The Israel Lobby* to downplay this enormous resource and grab all of the profits promised by U.S. corporate domination of those oil fields.

Obviously, oil is a big factor in the history of U.S. interventions in the Mideast, beginning with the 1953 overthrow in Iran of Mossadegh (whose crime was that he had begun nationalizing foreign-owned oil companies), and on through a policy centered on protecting the oil-rich despots in the Gulf. But oil isn't the only reason America has written itself militarily into the history books of other nations, often far more expansively than in the Mideast.

For example, the lack of oil or any other single vital resource in Vietnam was always a confusing fact when searching for a reason for that conflict, the most expensive war since World War II. That was particularly the case when anyone who spent even a small amount of time reading on the subject learned that the U.S. government's national security arguments about containing communism were all bogus. The Chinese communists were the inheritors of a thousand-year history of occupying Vietnam, and the Vietnamese communists were not about to act as their surrogates. Certainly after Richard Nixon, the great promoter of détente with the Soviets, extended that policy of reconciliation to China with his and Henry Kissinger's historic pilgrimage to Beijing, there was no rational excuse for staying in Vietnam. Yet millions more Indochinese and 30,000 more Americans died as the illogical war persisted, a war that had nothing to do with oil or any other U.S. national security interest.

The list of wars, or skirmishes, that never made any sense

economically or strategically during the Cold War is long and includes the hoary invocation of the Castro threat and the absurd Reagan war against tiny Grenada. Clinton's preoccupation with the splintering of Yugoslavia when he should have been dealing more intelligently and consistently with terrorism is another example, but there are dozens more. I bring this history up now to make the point that even the most pro-Israel of the neocon hawks, certainly Richard Perle and Paul Wolfowitz, were just as enthusiastic about conquering countries like Vietnam that had neither enemies of Israel nor oil. Nor were they driven by a desire to spread democracy as they have often proclaimed, since they have a long history of backing vicious dictators when convenient.

The common denominator in their target list for military-force projections was not a matter of religion, resources, or freedom, all of which may come into play from time to time, but rather that those targets presented an opportunity to flex American power and justify the real-life use of very complex and expensive war toys. The error commonly made in appraising the worldview of the military hawks is to take too seriously the stated goals of their policy, in other words, improving national security and spreading democracy. It is rather their means, the building of a war machine that they really care about as the source of prestige and profit, for them if not the nation.

Yes, in every instance they can make a case for war on other grounds—we stumbled in and can't just cut and run, the perception of our strength will be undermined, some sort of good outcome is just around the corner, and so on—but the harsh reality is that a cost-benefit analysis for the exercise of America's preparation for and conduct of war shows that it has been an enormous loser for the nation, needlessly sapping taxpayers, poisoning public life, and sacrificing soldiers. There is but one sector of American society that has benefited time and again from our grotesque waste of life and treasure, and it isn't the Israel lobby.

Trying to pin the Iraq war on a motivation that ignores the military-industrial complex just doesn't wash, whether the claimed motivation is Israel or oil. Israel, as we have seen and should have expected, was a big loser. The control of Gulf oil is even more problematic now as pipelines need to be guarded against insurgents, and anyway, even under the best of circumstances, the oil revenue will never pay for the cost of the war in American and Iraqi lives and U.S. taxpayer dollars. But the oil revenue is already a boon to the military contractors who, by the summer of 2007, had lined up billions in Iraq War–related weapons contracts.

No doubt invading a country with oil is better than taking over a country that has next to nothing in the way of natural resources, but the latter has most often been the norm, and those looking for an explanation for U.S. military adventures must explain this disparity in motives. Nor does the Zionist angle work, because it was absent in most cases. Of course, there are many forces driving an interventionist policy from exile communities in the United States, like the Cubans, to the let's-just-kick-someone's-ass-to-show-we're-alive approach, as in Reagan's invasion of little Grenada as though it were a rented movie set.

Most often those other explanations, while powerful in exceptional situations and moments, tend to lose their force when there are other pressing U.S. interests at stake. For example, there was a strong pro-Taiwan, anticommunist Chinese community in the United States that swore unending hostility to Red China, but when Nixon moved to embrace the Chinese communists in as abrupt a reversal of U.S. policy as is imaginable, the exile community quietly went along. So, too, with the large number of Vietnamese in the U.S., many of whom had arrived here after a harrowing journey as boat people but have since nonetheless adopted the prevailing U.S. government attitude toward a still-communist but free market–oriented Vietnam. Heated rhetoric aside, there are plenty of Vietnamese exiles who have returned home to their native villages to retire on their U.S. Social Security checks.

In short, when it suits the grander interest of the United States to abandon such causes, it is quite easily managed. Few, even in a media milieu inclined to be highly critical of Nixon, ever stopped to note the enormous contradiction of the old red-baiter still spewing the communists-are-coming-to-get-us line that launched him in politics to his last days in office while obsequiously cozying up to the Red Chinese government.

With regard to both China and Vietnam, the enormous shift in policy had precious little to do with changes in those regimes. Still quite boisterously communist in rhetoric at the time of rapprochement, the opening up of those societies came about after the United States moved from cold confrontation to warm diplomacy, not before. Militarism as the preferred means for containing those two nations gave way to diplomacy for the same reason that the more hawkish posture had been attractive: profit. Only now, as opposed to the earlier years of the Cold War, when a strong military posture seemed the best way to ensure defense profits at home and access to resources and markets abroad, has the U.S. found a better way. That way was demonstrated by the success of our economically developed allies in forging their own ties with China, generating considerable apprehension in the American business community that the potentially lucrative Chinese market, at the time containing more than one-fifth of the world's population, would be off limits to U.S. companies. Off limits as well for U.S. defense exports.

At the time of this writing as 2008 commences, I do not know how, or whether, the United States will extract itself from Iraq, thanks to Bush's obstinate desire to stumble upon victory. Perhaps he will, in the final throes of his power, take us into an even grander misadventure, such as invading Iran, although in December 2007 the National Intelligence Estimate—the consensus of the nation's sixteen intelligence centers—fundamentally challenged Bush's claims of the Iran threat. The NIE report concluded "with high confidence" that Iran had stopped its nuclear weapons program in 2003. The NIE's rare public rebuke of Bush was a stunning reminder that many of those in this country's elite with a say in foreign policy have rejected the neocon model of making the world safer and more profitable for America through the aggressive projection of military power. It has been exposed for what most foreign policy experts knew all along to be a nostalgic effort to reinvoke an old-fashioned imperialist model of direct control over nations and resources. But this would be neo-imperialism, so the control would be administered through meek surrogates.

The hard-bitten veterans of U.S. policy like those who followed Bush's father and his vision of a New World order, including Colin Powell, knew all along that the surrogate model wouldn't work. They, and others like them who had worked that gambit without success throughout the world, knew this before the neocons came up with the notion of installing pro-Western democracy in Iraq. The idea of casting Ahmed Chalabi as George Washington just reminded an earlier generation of dreamers that they had failed in attempting the same feat with Ngo Dinh Diem in Vietnam. Diem actually made it to South Vietnam's top office after he was ferried to Saigon from his exile residence in a Maryknoll seminary in New Jersey, but he was killed in a coup aided by the CIA after a decade of trying to administer Vietnam for the United States.

Today, American corporations have free access to exploit the productive labor of Vietnam, its main resource. The communist government even cooperates in suppressing those troublesome union-organizing movements, and there is no need for a massive military installation to guard American-owned factories. Sounds like a great deal for U.S. corporations, just as it has been in China, but not all will profit equally—and that's where we once again take up the sad plight of the military-industrial complex in the aftermath of Gorbachev's abdication of the Cold War. But first, a caveat for those readers who are scratching their heads and asking: but why can't aerospace companies like Boeing profit from commercial sales to participate in the development of countries like China instead of profiting from military equipment to contain them?

The answer is they can and they do. Boeing is an example of a company that has a very strong consumer market presence that is enhanced by peacetime conditions and threatened by military turmoil, as we witnessed with the steep nosedive of commercial aviation following the 9/11 terrorist attacks. Boeing did favor the opening to China and was early into that market, which caused some confusion for their favorite senator, Henry Jackson, who managed to shift his Cold War watch more directly toward the Soviet Union, which was not moving toward an open market available to Western companies.

It is fair to say that in companies like Boeing, there is a genuine tension between those whose sales boom with peace and the other branches whose weapons products require at least the dim possibility of war.

Not so most of the others in the defense industry, whose

business is more fully dependent on weapons sales. For example, Lockheed Martin, the biggest of the defense contractors, received 90 percent of its $41.9 billion in sales last year from such U.S. government contracts. Not to worry, as Kiplinger.com in February 2008 reported, the company has "a multiyear contract from the Air Force for sixty F-22 Raptor fighters," and then there is F-35: "The lifetime value of the company's contract to produce this jet is pegged at a whopping $300 billion."

Kilpinger quotes defense stock analyst Peter Arment as recommending a strong "buy" on Lockheed and offers as a reason for that optimism: "In the post 9/11 environment we believe national security issues will trump social causes, keeping the spending at elevated levels." He's right of course; the Bush administration proposed a $515 billion defense budget for 2009, 7.5 percent higher than for 2008 and with a cushy $184 billion for new weapons development and procurement. That $515 billion defense figure, as readers by now are no doubt tired of reading, does not include upward of an additional $200 billion for the Iraq and Afghanistan wars. So forget those social causes like better schools or improved health care.

For those naive enough to expect the presidential election to result in lower defense spending, Arment says don't believe it: "Defense stocks have historically outperformed in an election year, regardless of the outcome, as both parties talk about strong national security policies." That is, unless the public gets wise and stops buying the line that throwing hundreds of billions at airplanes we don't need has anything to do with national security. Some will profit, but on the whole, we lose big time.

Chapter 14

EMPIRE VS. REPUBLIC
—YOU DECIDE

War doesn't pay, nor does imperial ambition. That should be self-evident to anyone who has paid attention to the successful trajectory of the American experience, both politically and commercially, since the Republic's founding. It is a statement neither liberal nor conservative in orientation, and until recently it would have been accepted as a commonsense proposition by leading politicians of both political parties.

Although some leaders took us to war, they always claimed to do so reluctantly, as is reflected in the doubts expressed in their memoirs and those of their closest confidants. Lyndon Johnson, musing about the indefensibility of sacrificing even a single young American to die in Vietnam but sacrificing 59,000 of them in order to emerge victorious in his forthcoming election battle with Barry Goldwater, is all too typical. What that evidence reveals is just how intense is the political pressure to reject common sense when the specter of an enemy is raised. Those pressures have always been with us, and to the extent that they derive from national insecurities, political demagogues, economic avarice, overzealous patriotism, and religious or ideo-logical fervor, they are a constant of the human experience in just about any given society.

The amazing thing about the American political experi-ment is that our system is the one most consciously designed to limit those risks of foreign military adventure, and for most of our history, it has worked out quite well. I don't intend to minimize the expansionist, indeed rapacious conquest of our own continent, or the occasional colonial adventures abroad, as in the Philippines and other outposts from Hawaii to Alaska, but in the main, with few lapses, the public remained properly suspicious of its leaders' intentions. The dominant assumption was the importance of avoiding foreign "entanglements," to use Thomas Jefferson's words of warning about the risks of intervening in the affairs of others. Indeed, that policy of non-intervention was thought by our nation's founders to be a basic demarcation between the politics of the old and new worlds.

By nonintervention, they did not intend indifference to events in the outside world or a narrow protectionist view of trade accompanied by a fortress American military posture. Such a stance, often described as isolationism, obviously is not only out of joint with our current, highly interconnected world but it didn't make sense at the time of the nation's founding, even when the distance of oceans afforded far more secure borders than today. What nonintervention meant, as was com-monly understood even on the tavern bar level, was don't go sticking your nose into other people's business, and certainly don't pick fights that you can't finish. That is a posture that has nothing to do with limiting charitable concern for others be-yond your borders, missionary work abroad, humanitarian aid, and everything to do with avoiding the military expeditions that bankrupted the most pretentious and at times successful of empires. Not being like those empires was a driving force in the thinking of the nation's founders, who were in wide agreement on extreme caution as to military intervention.

That guiding idea of nonintervention—developed by the colonists in rebellion, espoused to great effect by the brilliant pamphleteer Thomas Paine, and crystallized as a national treasure in the final speech to the nation of George Washington—is as fresh and viable a construct as any of the great ideas that have guided our governance. Washington's Farewell Address, actually a carefully considered letter to the American people crafted in close consultation with Alexander Hamilton and James Madison, is one of our great treasures, but although read each year in the U.S. Senate to mark Washington's legacy, it contains a caution largely ignored by those same senators as they gleefully approve massive spending to enable international meddling of every sort. Their failed responsibility to limit the president's declaration of war has become a farce that as much as anything mocks Congress's obligations as laid out in the Constitution.

Explaining why he, as our first president, followed "our true policy to steer clear of permanent Alliances, with any portion of the foreign World. . . . Taking care always to keep ourselves, by suitable establishments on a respectably defensive posture," Washington shunned isolation, and instead held out a vision of peaceful international relations: "Harmony, liberal intercourse with all Nations, are recommended by policy, humanity and interest. But even our Commercial policy should hold an equal and impartial hand; neither seeking nor granting exclusive favors or preferences; consulting the natural course of things; diffusing and diversifying by gentle means the streams of commerce but forcing nothing."

What more powerful though gentle warning could be offered against the instincts to the imperial adventures that have destroyed all great empires? Washington knew this record of imperial folly well, and he was well aware that his countrymen could fall as had others for that siren song of military power coupled with economic greed that had humbled the powers of Europe: "In offering you, my Countrymen, these counsels of an old and affectionate friend . . . to moderate the fury of party spirit, to warn against the mischiefs of foreign Intrigue, to guard against the Impostures of pretended patriotism . . ."

What happened to us as a people that those modest yet profound sentiments now seem so foreign to the tongues of our politicians and the ears of their constituents? Who, be they Democrat or Republican, among our top leaders, particularly in the aftermath of the tragedy of 9/11, dares rise to warn against the "Impostures of pretended patriotism"? Are any of them as truly devoted as was Washington to "the benign influence of good Laws under a free Government," or indeed to the nurturing of what the founders well understood to be an ever fragile experiment in representative democracy?

For democracy to work, the scale must be kept small, and that is why the founders of the American version of that bold experiment stressed the local over the grand, leaving the majority of power to the individual and severely restricting the role of the state. To the degree that the state itself was tolerable, its power was severely curtailed, with the individual states of these United States reluctantly ceding the bare minimum of decision-making power necessary for the maintenance of public order to the new federal entity, one always to be regarded with the greatest of suspicion so widely shared and so obviously referenced in the original document that a Bill of Rights was not considered a necessity until the final draft of the Constitution.

If there is one thing that can be stated with absolute certainty as to their intentions, it is that the founders believed that the concepts of Republic and Empire represented an inevitable contradiction in terms. It is an essential caution that in the Cold War era came to be largely ignored. One reason is that our ambitions were never presented with the honesty of other imperial powers proclaiming their right to dominate others.

Our intrusions were always framed as defensive in nature, even when it meant dropping more explosives on the small country of Vietnam than had been dropped in all of World War II and leaving, according to Defense Secretary Robert McNamara, who initiated a good portion of the carnage, 3.4 million innocent dead in its wake. The policies were not conducted by a War Department, as had been the case during World War II, but rather a Department of Defense. So it has been with every U.S. military expedition of the past half century, efforts all conducted in the name of liberating others rather than feeding our delusions of grandeur, insecurities, and greed.

Of course, all empires have had their pretenses justifying the expansion of one nation's influence over others in the name of religion, freedom, combating aggression, or exporting the standards of higher civilization. There are elements of all that in what we do as a nation, but the compelling rubric that protects our adventures from internal criticism, though not necessarily from abroad, is that we seek no advantage for ourselves but only what is obviously good for others. Sometimes that may be the case, but it hardly works as an explanation of our enormously contradictory and often exploitative foreign policies.

However, it does work, at least in terms of creating a base of domestic political support for policies that in many instances contravene logic and fact. As Washington warned, it is extremely difficult to unmask the "Impostures of pretended patriotism" when the nation is frightened by enemies both real and imagined. Nor could Washington have anticipated the sort of mass media society in which government propaganda becomes compelling and inconvenient truths are easily concealed behind the veil of national security requirements. What he certainly did not anticipate is the modern militarized state, in which, ever since the onset of the Cold War a permanent war footing has been the norm for the first time in the nation's history.

For these reasons, the concerns of Washington expressed in his farewell speech needed the updating provided by the parting statement of our other great general turned president, Dwight David Eisenhower. Ike's Farewell Address provides a perfect bookend to that of Washington, for it marks a modern president's recognition that the fears of our first president had been realized. The empire had come to replace the republic. The "military-industrial complex" that Eisenhower warned against was merely the logical extension of an imperial reach of forward military bases throughout the world and a stark American intervention into the affairs of nations on every continent.

What alarmed him most is that while the enemy communism was in his mind all too real, the system that had grown up to counter it was self-perpetuating and disconnected from the defensive tasks at hand. Eisenhower predicted exactly what has come to pass. Despite the end of the Soviet Union, and with it the rationale for the Cold War, the military-industrial complex soon found another enemy, called terrorism.

The proof that Eisenhower's warnings were all too prescient is provided by the 2008 federal budget in which defense spending consumes $217 billion more than the total discretionary funding for all other divisions of the federal government. As Eisenhower warned:

> Our military organization today bears little relation to that known by any of my predecessors

in peace time, or indeed by the fighting men of World War II or Korea.

Until the latest of our world conflicts, the United States had no armaments industry. American makers of ploughshares could, with time as required, make swords as well. But now we can no longer risk emergency improvisation of national defense; we have been compelled to create a permanent armaments industry of vast proportions. . . .

This conjunction of an immense military establishment and a large arms industry is new in the American experience. The total influence—economic, political, even spiritual—is felt in every city, every state house, and every office of the federal government. We recognize the imperative need for this development. Yet we must not fail to comprehend its grave implications. . . .

In the councils of government, we must guard against the acquisition of unwarranted influence, whether sought or unsought, by the military-industrial complex. The potential for the disastrous rise of misplaced power exists and will persist.

We must never let the weight of this combination endanger our liberties or democratic processes. We should take nothing for granted; only an alert and knowledgeable citizenry can compel the proper meshing of huge industrial and military machinery of defense with our peaceful methods and goals, so that security and liberty may prosper together.

There you have it; don't say we weren't warned. Mind you, Eisenhower was willing to speak out against this "unwarranted influence" at a time when he thought there was an equally powerful adversary equipped with precisely the same sort of advanced weaponry as we possessed. There was a high-tech arms race underway, and yet even then Eisenhower sounded his warning. What is the excuse of politicians and the media for not sounding that warning when we face no such adversary but yet defense spending is at an obscene all-time high?

The disconnect between the arsenal of the terrorist enemy and that which has been arrayed against it in the post-9/11 years more than affirms Eisenhower's warning about the "unwarranted influence" of the military-industrial complex. The good news, however, is that it derives from a power base fraught with contradictions. As we have seen in this book, much of what is demanded by the military machine is absurdly disproportionate to the task at hand. One wonders how the lobbyists and politicians even maintain a straight face as they argue, as did Senator Lieberman, for $2.5 billion submarines to fight terrorists without even a dingy. I don't doubt that they will continue to make their case and that the money spent toward that end will secure political and pundit support, but it is wearing thin. So, too, the effort to manufacture crises with "rogue nations" and to continuously exaggerate the cohesion and power of the "terrorist" enemy. Nor will the Chinese- or the Russians-are-coming gambit work as both of those countries move deeper into the fray of the commercial markets rather than serving as props in the theater of war games.

The U.S. military budget is roughly equal to that of all of the rest of the world's nations, and it is inconceivable that any hostile state could emerge in the next twenty years with the ability to match the United States in a combat zone, even if no new weapons are added to the American arsenal. It is also true that we can likely go on building unneeded weapons systems without destroying our overall economy. While the budget is almost twice as large as it was in Eisenhower's last year in constant dollars, it is half of what it was as a percentage of Gross Domestic Product. The good news in that statistic is that it should be easier to eliminate defense-related jobs without having as much negative impact on the economy as in Eisenhower's time.

The benefits of such a cut would be more dramatic in freeing up government funds for other purposes, including programs in health and education that would make the nation stronger. The reality is that there is no will in the United States in either party to raise taxes, and as a result, existing and new programs must compete for a fixed pool of tax dollars. The dollars that can be allocated are further limited because of mandatory expenditures, including the two largest—Social Security and Medicare—which will not be cut because of the voter resentment that would ensue. For these reasons, the full range of nonmandated programs, all those items that are wrangled over by Congress from farm subsidies through children's health insurance and medical research are competing with the defense dollar, which is almost totally discretionary.

Therefore, the essential parameter in considering how we allocate federal funds boils down to what is available in the discretionary spending category, where roughly six out of ten dollars go to the military side. As a consequence, it is from cutbacks on military spending that funding will in all likelihood have to be found for increases in domestic spending. That is the most honest way to judge the opportunity cost of the defense dollar, as in two unneeded submarines versus coverage of health insurance for four million kids.

There is, however, a greater cost to a huge permanent military to which Eisenhower was alluding, and that concerns the vitality of our democracy. As we saw in the run-up to the Iraq war, the threat inflators who seek an expanded military role are not above using their enormous lobbying power to influence the political debate and votes in Congress. If the military were merely a boondoggle in which defense contractors, top military officers, and all those who work in the defense bureaucracy and industry were simply viewed as recipients of an enormously bountiful welfare program, the costs to the society, as measured in dollar payments, would arguably be manageable. Some, like Colin Powell in his autobiography, even defend the armed forces as a purveyor of enlightened social services, particularly in affording education and job training to those who failed to obtain needed skills from the public schools. If one could restrict the military to that sort of function, it might be duplicitous but defensible as a needed social program.

The problem is that the public will not support the military unless it feels that its activities are connected with a real threat, and as a result the military and its suppliers and other allies have a built-in need to exaggerate the threat. That is the risk of "the total influence—economic, political, even spiritual" that Eisenhower warned is "felt in every city, every state house, every office of the federal government." It is a built-in and well-financed constituency for stressing the military option over the diplomatic one, for exaggerating the strength of the enemy rather than realistically appraising it, and for finding new wars to be fought with a sense of desperation. While it is certainly true that there are those in the military hierarchy resistant to military engagements that cannot be won—Colin Powell is an example—it is also true that warriors need wars in order to establish their relevance. So, too, the national security experts in the think tanks who do much to shape the national agenda.

No need, however, to get too gloomy here, for the bottom line is that even most of the hawks could find something else to do for a living, and we do have examples of former imperial powers decommissioning their military force, as we did after both World Wars, and rising to higher levels of prosperity. That indeed was the direction in which we were headed after the first President Bush acknowledged the end of the Cold War, and few would deny that the economy fared far better during the years of much lower defense spending during the Clinton administration than as a result of the defense spending spree of the George W. Bush presidency. It is also true that those spending levels of the Clinton years left the United States strong enough to easily conquer Afghanistan and Iraq, although the lengthy occupation of both countries has proved far more burdensome.

The short answer is that we can have peace and prosperity, and we can easily afford to cushion the fall for those who have grown dependent on the defense dollar. It means, however, not invading countries that we have to occupy at great cost, a lesson that the American public, which gave Bush a blank check, now at last seems to have learned.

So, yes, there is much reason to hope that the military buildup of the George W. Bush years is an aberration, since the objective reality out there—the utter lack of credible enemies with advanced weaponry—makes it an increasingly difficult sell. Yet as I write those words, I hear again Eisenhower's warning and wonder if I am not being overly optimistic. Yes, the money we are spending is absurdly disproportionate to the task at hand, the weapons are making us less secure, not more so, powerful forces are unleashed that seek to find excuse for war, and we are dramatically increasing a fiscal debt that will deprive future generations of needed government services and programs. What is going on in our name is irrational, costly, and dangerous, but there are powerful vested interests that want to keep it that way.

Will they win? You decide.

AFTERWORD

The storm clouds have parted, maybe. In the afterglow of the departure of George W. Bush there is cause for renewed optimism in matters of war and peace. The deadly hubris of the neoconservatives has been soundly rejected, and common sense about the limits of American power seems to have been restored.

With attention now shifted to the economic meltdown, there is the hope that resources wasted on military expansion will be diverted, out of necessity as well as logic, to solving our pressing economic problems. If ever there was a time to beat swords into plowshares, this is it.

Clearly, we are in an era of limits in which the federal government's resources must be husbanded. Trillions wasted during the Bush years to defeat a terrorist enemy whose arsenal could be obtained for a few hundred bucks at Home Depot are now needed to avert a collapse of our financial system that represents a far graver threat to our nation's security than the ragtag remnants of al Qaeda.

That we cannot continue to spend more than half of the federal discretionary budget on superexpensive but irrelevant Cold War–era weapons has been recognized by the Obama administration. The president's pledge to cut the deficit by the end of his term, despite the enormous cost of the financial bailout and stimulus packages, is, as he stated, contingent on dramatically cutting the cost of foreign military interventions, beginning with the Iraq occupation.

But will Obama, elected as he was on a promise of challenging the imperial overreach of the Bush administration, manage to resist the enduring pressure from the military-industrial complex to find excuses to go to war?

He has rejected Bush's reliance on unilateral militarism, promoting instead multilateralism and diplomacy and an end to the excesses of the imperial presidency. Most important, he promises an honest transparency in the conduct of his presidency, and that transformation, if applied to the machinations of the military-industrial complex, could spell its doom.

But it won't be easy. As Eisenhower warned, and as readers of this book are now no doubt tired of reading, the military economy has a life of its own quite apart from the objective threats to the nation's security and whichever party happens to be in power. After all, as discussed in chapter two, when Donald Rumsfeld assumed control of the Pentagon, he too viewed it as a beast to be tamed. Recall the speech delivered on the day before 9/11, in which Rumsfeld bravely challenged unbridled military spending as the nation's greatest threat. Then a day later, as we know too well, such cautions evaporated and Rumsfeld and the president he served, who had been elected on a promise of lower government budgets, launched a military buildup of unprecedented proportions. In Bush's final year annual defense spending was higher than in any year during the Cold War.

But even during the last years of the Bush administration, that misallocation of resources had begun to be questioned by the man who replaced Rumsfeld as secretary of defense. Robert Gates had dared challenge some of the most egregious examples of outdated priorities, particularly the obsession with the F-22 stealth fighter, which had not flown a single combat mission in Iraq, Afghanistan, or anywhere else. The $65 billion F-22 program had produced a plane that was used primarily for ceremonial functions like flying over a championship college football game.

Gates even went so far as to fire the top military and civilian officials in the Air Force for their zeal in pushing for more of these planes, though the Pentagon did not even want them. Perhaps now, as Obama's secretary of defense, Gates will make good on curtailing the F-22 and some other high-profile weapons systems that he has strenuously observed are useless in the sort of asymmetrical low-tech wars against terrorism and the like that are in the offing.

Or perhaps not. In the months between Obama's election and his inauguration, defense hawks in Congress ramped up commitments for the F-22 and, as had become the fashion in the midst of the economic meltdown that Obama inherited, it was now presented as a jobs program. So too the other high-tech weapons systems that had little if anything to do with meeting any current or foreseeable dangers.

A month before Barack Obama was inaugurated as the forty-fourth president, the Democratic leadership in Congress sent a signal that, as far as the military-industrial complex was concerned, it would be business as usual. With no shortage of Republican allies, they voted to spend $14 billion more on new Virginia-class submarines, discussed in chapter seven, a ludicrous weapon in a war to vanquish terrorists based in the landlocked region straddling the Pakistan-Afghanistan border.

As was noted earlier in this book, the Democrats originally came to support an expansion of submarine production because they are primarily produced in Groton, Connecticut. That happens to be a swing district whose election of Democrat Joe

Courtney by a scant eighty-three-vote margin in the 2006 election was one of the victories needed for the Democrats to gain control of the House of Representatives.

Courtney, embraced by the Democratic leadership in the person of Pennsylvania's Jack Murtha, who chairs the House Appropriations Defense Subcommittee, soon acquired even more money for the sub program than his Republican predecessor and was easily reelected. Not taking any chances on the preferences of the new Democratic president, Courtney, with Murtha's powerful backing, pushed Congress to commit to the biggest expenditure ever on new subs even before Obama was sworn in.

An editorial in the *New York Times* a week before the vote to expand the program had called for ending it: "Halt production of the Virginia-class sub . . . The program is little more than a public works project to keep the Newport News, Va., and Groton, Conn., naval shipyards in business."

As Connecticut Senator Joe Lieberman, a huge backer of the subs, boasted, "I'm proud that the Virginia-class submarines are built in Groton, Connecticut, supporting thousands of good jobs in our region." In the midst of an economic meltdown, the claimed job-creation power of defense spending became the central argument for expenditures that could not be justified in terms of national security.

What irony then that a proposal a month later to save many more General Motors autoworkers' jobs at a lower cost was the subject of intense congressional debate. If GM executives had come hat in hand offering to build more military-outfitted Hummers, they would have been granted a more receptive hearing.

Of course, weapons can't be marketed simply as a jobs program, and Lieberman and Courtney continued to make the case that the subs are needed to counter a potential threat from China. What is so odd about that argument is that the financial meltdown brought the Chinese Communists to the fore of the discussion, not as a military enemy to be defeated but as the holders of a major portion of our foreign debt. The threat from the Chinese was not in their potential subs, but rather that they might sell their trillion dollars in U.S. treasury notes. And in any case, what did the Chinese have to do with the terrorist attack on the United States, which was the occasion of the post–Cold War spending spree?

Don't look for a rational connection. It is yet another sad example of how the specter of foreign danger is employed to mask other objectives of political ambition and greed.

Can Obama break that dependency? While he has challenged the Bush orthodoxy in the "war on terror," Obama in his first months as president seemed bent on repeating the mistakes. While attempting to disengage from the quagmire of Iraq, the new president quickly plunged into the far more treacherous one in Afghanistan. Once again, the complex history of another nation was being subsumed to the simplistic rhetoric of American politics, and the military option was expanded before the political alternatives were even superficially probed.

The good news is that the Afghan war provides even less in the way of an excuse for a buildup in high-tech weaponry than could be found in Saddam Hussein's Iraq. Recall Donald Rumsfeld's plaintive argument for invading Iraq, stating that there "are no good targets in Afghanistan." Saddam Hussein's regime had been demonized, particularly in the neoconservative literature, as a modernized military force armed with weapons of mass destruction, and analogies were drawn with the rise of Hitler's Germany. As nonsensical as such a comparison was, it seemed all the more absurd if one attempted to defend the development of an ultrasophisticated U.S. military machine to combat the primitively armed forces of the Taliban.

The problem facing the high-tech military-industrial complex is that in a world torn by asymmetrical warfare, the expensive military equipment is just not useful, even as a means of advancing imperial overreach. And to use the phrase from that *New York Times* editorial, as "a public works project," it is wildly inefficient as a jobs creator. High-tech weaponry requires spending a disproportionate amount of money on expensive materials, computer code, and robotics, and relatively less on labor. As a jobs program, it can't compare with following John Maynard Keynes's alternative of simply paying the unemployed to dig holes and then fill them up. Or better yet, paying folks to build a green economy.

That is why the lobbyists for the military-industrial complex, as well-financed and creative as they may be, will not win the argument for a bigger military as a means of reversing the economic meltdown. There are just too many better ways to spend that money. What they, and their allies, must do to make the case for a huge peacetime military is to find wars to fight abroad even when they make no sense. And therein lies the danger from a military-industrial complex that remains unchecked.

There is already a disturbing undertone in the debate over dealing with the economic meltdown. While Obama stresses that he is operating in the activist tradition of Franklin Roosevelt's New Deal, his critics, almost all of the Congressional Republican delegation and its talk radio gurus, insist that the New Deal failed to end the depression and that only the entrance of the United States into World War II brought the country back to prosperity.

That argument is as wrong as it is ominous. Wrong because

Roosevelt's programs clearly helped stabilize the economy, and the evidence is that his New Deal spending programs were effective but needed to be larger in scope rather than abandoned in principle. Clearly, the multiplier effect of a dollar spent on the domestic side has a more favorable impact on job creation than when appropriated to the military. But what makes the war-equals-prosperity argument ominous is its implied assumption that we will never summon the national will to make the right public investments unless it is for war.

If that is the case, then the hope of our nation's founders for a peaceable republic employing primarily what George Washington referred to as "gentle means" will be crushed. If we can only act with a strong sense of national purpose in the face of an exaggerated foreign threat and not, as our founders intended, to deal primarily with pressing domestic issues of national commerce such as the banking crisis, then our Republic will come to be judged as a failed experiment. A political and economic system that requires war for its salvation is not worth preserving. Fortunately, there are peaceful alternatives that would create jobs and preserve democracy.

ACKNOWLEDGMENTS

This book would not exist without the efforts of my son Joshua Scheer, who did the heavy lifting on the research and, with his encyclopedic memory of weapons and key players, very much helped to shape its focus, particularly as to the egregious examples of waste, which he unearthed with a zeal inspired by his libertarian bent. Although not convinced to support Ron Paul, I have to admit that folks on that side of the political spectrum have done as much as anyone to reign in the enormous expansion of government power reflected in the military budget.

Indeed, the idea for this book was born with a speech I gave to the libertarian Future of Freedom Foundation, a broadcast of which caught the attention of my editor, Jonathan Karp. He suggested I write this book when I came to him with another book project, which in retrospect would have been far less important. I thank him for his wisdom and patience. The two other participants in that meeting, my book agent and friend Steve Wasserman and my coworker Kasia Anderson, deserve a great deal of credit for the book's original conception. Anderson, who is completing her doctorate at USC, where we team teach, has been a major force in guiding the project, holding me to deadlines, and providing skillful editing. She managed to improve my book copy while helping edit Truthdig.com, which, thanks in part to her efforts, won the 2007 Webby for the Internet's best political blog.

Major credit for Truthdig, as well as help on this book, is very much due to Peter Scheer, who as Truthdig managing editor kept the site going, freeing me to work on this book, and who also managed to find time to make this book better with his expert editing. As opposed to Joshua, Peter weighed in on the side of caution as to my tendency to excessively praise John McCain and anyone else in government who seemed concerned about wasting taxpayers' dollars. Peter constantly reminded me that it hardly made sense to have advocated restraints on military spending while voting in favor of the invasion of Iraq and the escalation of the U.S. military presence, as McCain did.

My three sons have been a constant source of instruction and inspiration. My oldest, Christopher Scheer, has been my cowriter on movies including Oliver Stone's *Nixon* and the book *The Five Biggest Lies Bush Told Us about Iraq*, where I received cowriting credit for a work that was largely his. This time, it was the turn of my younger sons Joshua and Peter to carry me, and I am grateful that the louts turned out so well. Zuade Kaufman, my publisher at Truthdig, deserves the main credit for the site's success and has been enormously supportive of me in every possible way. Zuade, who began her journalism career working with me on my local *Los Angeles Times* columns and later joined me in launching Truthdig after obtaining her master's in journalism at USC, is a model of journalistic excellence and integrity.

Finding time to write this book while carrying on the duties of my day job teaching in the Annenberg School for Communication at the University of Southern California was made possible by my department chair, tough intellectual critic and good friend Larry Gross, who made room for me to publish without perishing. And special thanks go to Barbra Frank and John Cheney-Lippold for meticulous copyediting and fact-checking.

Too many of us on the left have tended to accommodate military spending as a benign jobs program rather than the enabler of death and destruction that is its organic intention. Some liberals like George McGovern got it right, and for that and other reasons I am much in debt to his example. I reread Stephen Ambrose's book dealing with the heroic World War II efforts of McGovern that earned him the Distinguished Flying Cross in order to remind myself of the depths of deceit of the false patriots like Richard Nixon, who besmirched McGovern's patriotism, while they, mostly chicken hawks who avoided combat, sent others to die. Not so the other leader to whom I dedicated this book, the general who became president Dwight David Eisenhower, whom I admired as a man of peace after he brought Soviet leader Nikita Khrushchev to the United States, thereby demystifying the enemy on both sides of the Cold War.

While she was not a war hero, my wife, Narda Zacchino, was conceived through the union of two WWII marines, Pete Zacchino and Helen Wenzak Zacchino, and they passed on to their children a strong belief that war should only be fought to ensure peace and not as an end in itself. Everyone who has known Narda in her professional capacity as the associate editor of the *Los Angeles Times*, where we both worked for a combined sixty years, or later as the deputy editor of the *San Francisco Chronicle*, knows that Narda is not responsible for any of the errors in this book (she doesn't make them) and for much of what is worthwhile. She married way down, and for that I am very grateful. Narda found time to help me enormously on this book while helping run the *San Francisco Chronicle* and working with Mary Tillman on her incredibly moving book in tribute to her son Patrick. Their efforts to untangle the web of the government's lies was a constant reminder to me that militarism is not a game to be played for fun and profit.

INDEX

ABOUT THE AUTHOR

ROBERT SCHEER is currently editor in chief of Truthdig.com, 2007 Webby Award winner for best political blog. He is also a contributing editor for *The Nation*; a syndicated columnist based at the *San Francisco Chronicle*; and a host of *Left, Right & Center* on KCRW, the NPR affiliate in Santa Monica. Between 1964 and 1969 he was a Vietnam correspondent and editor in chief of *Ramparts* magazine. He spent twenty-nine years at the *Los Angeles Times* as a national reporter, columnist, and contributing editor. He was also a project consultant for Oliver Stone's *Nixon* and played the role of a journalist in Warren Beatty's *Bullworth*. He is the author of seven books, including *With Enough Shovels: Reagan, Bush & Nuclear War*. He can be reached via www.Truthdig.com.

ABOUT TWELVE

TWELVE was established in August 2005 with the objective of publishing no more than one book per month. We strive to publish the singular book, by authors who have a unique perspective and compelling authority. Works that explain our culture; that illuminate, inspire, provoke, and entertain. We seek to establish communities of conversation surrounding our books. Talented authors deserve attention not only from publishers, but from readers as well. To sell the book is only the beginning of our mission. To build avid audiences of readers who are enriched by these works—that is our ultimate purpose.

For more information about forthcoming TWELVE books, please go to www.TwelveBooks.com.